W9-ADR-633

THE ENLIGHTENMENT

MAJOR ISSUES IN HISTORY

Editor

C. WARREN HOLLISTER

University of California, Santa Barbara

THE ENLIGHTENMENT

EDITED BY

Leonard M. Marsak

University of California, Santa Barbara

John Wiley & Sons, Inc.

New York • London • Sydney • Toronto

Library of Congress Cataloging in Publication Data

Marsak, Leonard Mendes, 1924-   comp.
   The Enlightenment.

   (Major issues in history)
   Bibliography: p.
   1. Enlightenment. 2. Philosophy, Modern—18th century. I. Title.

B802.M36   190'.9'033   72-2444
ISBN 0-471-57280-2
ISBN 0-471-57281-0 (pbk.)

Printed in the United States of America

10 9 8 7 6 5 4 3 2 1

SERIES PREFACE

The reading program in a history survey course traditionally has consisted of a large two-volume textbook and, perhaps, a book of readings. This simple reading program requires few decisions and little imagination on the instructor's part, and tends to encourage in the student the virtue of careful memorization. Such programs are by no means things of the past, but they certainly do not represent the wave of the future.

The reading program in survey courses at many colleges and universities today is far more complex. At the risk of oversimplification, and allowing for many exceptions and overlaps, it can be divided into four categories: (1) textbook, (2) original source readings, (3) specialized historical essays and interpretive studies, and (4) historical problems.

After obtaining an overview of the course subject matter (textbook), sampling the original sources, and being exposed to selective examples of excellent modern historical writing (historical essays), the student can turn to the crucial task of weighing various possible interpretations of major historical issues. It is at this point that memory gives way to creative critical thought. The "problems approach," in other words, is the intellectual climax of a thoughtfully conceived reading program and is, indeed, the most characteristic of all approaches to historical pedagogy among the newer generation of college and university teachers.

The historical problems books currently available are many and varied. Why add to this information explosion? Because the Wiley Major Issues Series constitutes an endeavor to produce something new that will respond to pedagogical needs thus far unmet. First, it is a series of individual volumes—one per problem. Many good teachers would much prefer to select their own historical issues rather than be tied to an inflexible sequence of issues imposed by a publisher and bound together between two covers. Second, the Wiley Major Issues Series is based on the idea of approaching the significant problems of history through a deft interweaving of primary sources and secondary analysis, fused together by the skill of a scholar-editor. It is felt that the essence of a historical issue cannot be satisfactorily probed either by placing a body of undigested source materials into the hands of inexperienced students or by limiting these students to the controversial literature of modern scholars who debate the meaning of sources the student never sees. This series approaches historical problems by exposing students to both the finest historical thinking on the issue and some of the evidence on which this thinking is based. This synthetic approach should prove far more fruitful than either the raw-source approach or the exclusively second-hand approach, for it combines the advantages—and avoids the serious disadvantage—of both.

Finally, the editors of the individual volumes in the Major Issues Series have been chosen from among the ablest scholars in their fields. Rather than faceless referees, they are historians who know their issues from the inside and, in most instances, have themselves contributed significantly to the relevant scholarly literature. It has been the editorial policy of this series to permit the editor-scholars of the individual volumes the widest possible latitude both in formulating their topics and in organizing their materials. Their scholarly competence has been unquestioningly respected; they have been encouraged to approach the problems as they see fit. The titles and themes of the series volumes have been suggested in nearly every case by the scholar-editors themselves. The criteria have been (1) that the issue be of relevance to undergraduate lecture courses in history, and (2) that it be an issue which the scholar-editor knows thoroughly and in which he has done creative work. And, in general, the second criterion has been given precedence over the first. In short, the question "What are the significant historical issues today?" has been answered not by general editors or sales departments but by the scholar-teachers who are responsible for these volumes.

University of California,　　　　　　　　　　*C. Warren Hollister*
Santa Barbara

CONTENTS

THE ENLIGHTENMENT

PART ONE

The Enlightenment

1   INTRODUCTION:
THE ENLIGHTENMENT—WHAT WAS IT?

The Enlightenment was perhaps the end of the Renaissance or of the Middle Ages, or else the beginning of modern times, as some have argued, but there can be no doubt about its essential character. It was an age of secular or scientific humanism. It drew sustenance from the seventeenth-century accomplishments in science and reason, but its chief concerns were for ethics and social thought. It was the last great age of political theory, and we have been living off its ideas until the present, when in all aspects of public life they are in retreat.

The Enlightenment was the work of the *philosophes*—the intellectuals who made it. They are known by the French word because the Enlightenment was primarily a French phenomenon, although there was an English and German Enlightenment as well, and additional expressions of the movement in Italy, Spain, and in America. While it is possible to speak of national enlightenments, for there were particular varieties of thought in response to each country's circumstances, there was nonetheless a common intellectual experience in eighteenth-century Europe that is possible to define.

The *philosophes* looked to science and exploration not so much for new knowledge, although that certainly figured in their thought, as for new attitudes toward knowledge. They borrowed from science the skeptical attitude of systematic doubt, and from exploration a new relativist attitude toward belief, and used them to discredit traditional religious and political values as so many ethnocentric convictions to be discarded for their prejudice, dogmatism, and intolerance. Montesquieu's tolerant Persians, Voltaire's sage Chinese, Diderot's virtuous Tahitians, coming after Fontenelle's plurality of worlds, that was designed to reduce man in his pride, all served as useful devices for criticizing European society and suggesting a better one. Curiously, the effect of such skepticism and relativism was to magnify man in general and European man in particular.

Skepticism and relativism were strengthened for the *philosophes* by the methodological concerns of the preceding century. The scientific spokesmen of that century—Francis Bacon, René Descartes, John Locke, and Isaac Newton—all appealed for a rational standard of truth that subsequently, in the work of the eighteenth century, would do away with metaphysics and miracles, declare nature uniform, and knowledge provisional, contingent upon man and the way he goes about securing it, and redounding to his benefit. What emerged from this intellectual activity were the words nature, reason, man, and progress which became a medium of exchange among thinking men and which were used to forge a scientific humanism. Laws of nature were viewed as existing within nature, allowing nature to be self-sustaining, free from the intervention of a capricious and personal god. Reason, however defined, was that capacity in man to understand the behavior of nature under law, and so to come to terms with it. Reason could be viewed as god's purest revelation to man, the source of all knowledge; or as an objective standard for truth signifying the reasonableness of belief when achieved in compliance with the rules of evidence. D'Alembert demonstrated in the *Encyclopaedia* the proposition that positive knowledge, won by reason, answered pragmatically to man's needs and contributed to scientific and social progress, now made possible by the discovery of nature's laws, which reason itself expresses. Progress in thought or activity is inconceivable in a world deemed random and chaotic, where man is without history, subject to an arbitrary fate that is often cruelly capricious. History and progress were thus firmly linked in the minds of the *philosophes,* and man's future state described as the increase of reason and freedom.

Their quest for freedom, whether viewed politically in Locke's fashion as freedom from restraint, or morally in Rousseau's fashion, implying constraint, was predicated on devising a secular ethic to substitute for the traditional one judged no longer viable under the impact of science. In the absence of the Christian god the source and sanction for behavior was found in reason. Reason not only secured knowledge for man, but was also a source of goodness in him; for reason is a faculty common to man everywhere that allows him to cut away what is merely customary in his life, to discover his essential humanity, and so to join with others in universal brotherhood. Whether it was Cartesian reason they relied on, or Humean reasonableness, their definition of the word reflected their scientific experience. The first way of reason provided a degree of certainty, sought by Kant, that was unobtainable by the second route, more probabilistic in character, and lending itself to a utilitarian ethic. Kantian or utilitarian, however, the *philosophes* believed that the good has its uses, and not the converse, that what is useful to man is necessarily good. The utilitarian ethic, concerned with *consequences*, was designed to calculate principles of reasonable behavior in society. Kant's rationalist ethic, emphasizing intention, was devised to satisfy the requirements of a higher pragmatism, namely the practicality of a rational foundation for morality. In sum, enlightenment ethics of both varieties had their source in science; they were accordingly experimental in character and not merely experiential; that is, they did not answer simply to man's impulses. Finally, both varieties had as their goal the improvement of man's lot on earth and not in heaven.

The *philosophes* undercut traditional religion but were by no means agreed on what they would have instead. They argued the relative merits of a natural religion, a rational one, one based on feeling, or none at all. Although they all assumed an order to nature they could not agree on the fundamental meaning of nature's laws, as expressing primarily truth, or beauty, or goodness. They had no logical surety about man. If man is defined in natural terms, and nature is good, whence evil? From unnatural men, they answered, involving themselves in a logical dilemma they tried to resolve in a number of ways, all of which begged the question. In the end, they decided that the essential task is not to define man's nature, but to alter society in the hope of changing his behavior. But they had no common convictions about the forms or specific virtues of society. Montesquieu sought liberty in an aristocratic society, Voltaire order and efficiency in a reformed monarchy, and Rousseau equality in a democracy. They were all agreed, however, that man is an autonomous being who might rise above nature to secure the blessings of freedom in a progressive society.

Central to all shadings of ethical thought during the Enlightenment was the eighteenth-century idea of progress. The *philosophes* believed that social progress is promoted by science in stages of increasing refinement: from material progress to the progress of knowledge, to the progress of the mind through the increase of reason. While the findings of science reduced men's ignorance, it was the method of science which freed their minds from error and superstition, thereby freeing them, as it did the scientist, of prejudice, dogmatism, and intolerance. The *philosophes* found in the scientific experience the qualities of a progressive society. In addition they discovered the uses of history.

If the growth of science has governed man's progress in the past, and science is defined in terms of its method, then the method of science is the principle of explanation in history. Given the undoubted fact of scientific progress, it is clear that we have made such progress in history, that is to say, in process. Progress is what distinguishes us from the past; process implies that we have continuity with the past, and also with the future. Thus we can look to the future with hope for those good things, both mental and material, that will relieve man's age-old burdens. But the man who opts for progress must choose among social and political alternatives, and in so doing the obligation to think clearly is a moral one. Not that the *philosophes* denied the emotions or relied exclusively on reason. (In fact they sought to limit reason for in that way is its essential structure preserved.) Instead, the Enlightenment argued for the preeminence of reason while speaking for the primacy of ethics, for only by the exercise of man's reason is the ethical life sustained. The identification of man's reason with his freedom was complete.

For the *philosophes* science was therefore a hopeful creed that had revolutionary implications. Their support of science was concerned with the perfection of society only as it promotes each man's purpose: the increase of freedom and equality, and not the purpose of some collective entity, unless it be mankind as a whole. The *philosophes* thought that men control their own destiny. They did not talk of necessary perfection, but of the capacity in men for earthly perfection, perceiving that while science must serve an ethical purpose, ethics must not be modeled on scientific laws. To do so would be to misread both science and ethics, and thus in scientific fashion to define *as* history what must be accomplished by men *in* history. History and science do not guarantee the betterment of man, but only provide him with the time and setting in which to be moral. By insisting on the autonomy of human reason, the Enlightenment gave to each man the responsibility for moral and social decision, together with a sense of historical time that saw history as a continuum of moments objectively equal in time, in which each moment may be subjectively heightened by the sum of lived experience, personal and historical. The millenarian conceives the moment otherwise; as the sum of all time contained in one lived experience. The Age of Reason based history on objective, scientific time, while congruently it historicized science. The *philosophes* would not have shared the present fondness for doing without history and finding values in togetherness, now.

For a long time scholars were of the opinion that the *philosophes* merely popularized the intellectual achievements of the seventeenth century. It seems reasonable to argue, however, that in taking hold of the seventeenth century victories for reason and science, and in extending them to man and society, the *philosophes* created a new world view that was indeed a philosophy in its own right. The Enlightenment borrowed from the literary humanism of the Renaissance and by the addition of science gave it force and direction. The *philosophes'* skepticism was not the negative variety of the Renaissance Pyrrhonist who believed there is nothing we can know with any assurance; but the positive kind of the scientist whose discipline requires him to generalize from observable fact, with the historical consequence of scientific and social progress. Thus knowledge that is said to spring from man, may now redound to his social benefit. Renaissance humanism, which might augment the dignity of the individual, was newly directed toward society in a humanitarian venture designed to raise the intellectual and material well-being of humanity as a whole. For the first time since antiquity the sciences and humanities were successfully linked in thought, and the humanist and humanitarian impulses joined in a concern for each individual, and not for individualism, which consigns the majority of individuals to oblivion. There were tensions that existed even then between the humanist and humanitarian impulses; tensions that are being very clearly expressed today by social scientists who, in the name of humanitarianism, are attacking both science and the humanities, and who as heirs of the Enlightenment thereby exemplify the old belief that the child devours the parent. But for at least a century, from about 1750 to 1850, men believed that they held the two impulses in dynamic equilibrium. By translating humanist-scientific values of skepticism, relativism, and pragmatism into social values of tolerance, free thought, and rational consent, the *philosophes* hoped to persuade mankind to abolish pride of ignorance, to be satisfied with less than absolute certainty of knowledge, and to enter history, in the belief that the willingness to do these things is not only a characteristic of the intellectual but a mark of the civilized man.

. . .

It is not our intention in this anthology to offer a catalogue of writers in small selections to cover all aspects of the Enlightenment, but to include a few representative figures in large selections, and to keep each man's work together under one of three headings that illustrate the major concerns of the age. Those headings are the themes of the Enlightenment: Reason and Nature, Man and Morals, Politics and Progress. Each of the *philosophes* presented wrote on all three subjects, and in the selections included here touch on two at least. The *Philosophical Dictionary* may be listed under man as well as reason. In the case of Rousseau's work it is difficult to distinguish between politics and morality. Even so it is reasonable to reserve each writer for a particular heading in order to show first, the emphasis he gave to his work, and second, the topical development to Enlightenment thought that was most characteristic of it. In this way we may proceed from considerations of right thinking, to those of right acting, and to the expression of both in programs for social betterment, as the eighteenth century did.

The second part of the volume speaks for itself. In the conclusion we consider the relevance or irrelevance of the Enlightenment, now past, but which like all periods of history may have something of value to offer us if we understand it sufficiently to profit by it. Knowledge won in other times and circumstances may be true knowledge for all that, and significant to us providing we choose to make it so. As the *philosophes* knew, those who are without affective memory are subject to mental disorder. The future has meaning only in reference to the past, so that effort made toward progress may be the ultimate conservative act. Conversely, the true radicals among us may be the beasts of the field, who do not go forward because they never go back, and for whom each moment, identical to the one preceding, is always radically new.

A. REASON AND NATURE

1   *Montesquieu*

Charles Louis de Secondat, Baron de Montesquieu (1689–1755), was born of an honorable family of magistrates. Though Montesquieu himself was conservative in outlook, his work has served to justify various political positions. In The Persian Letters *(1721) he pleads for liberty and toleration, and details the arguments for natural religion and a virtue ethic, themes synonymous with the Enlightenment.* The Spirit of the Laws *(1748) seems to have as its premise that truth and justice, based on reason, are universal—a belief that went well with his cosmopolitanism.*

Montesquieu's reasoning, however, led him to a political relativism sometimes at odds with his premises. The value of civil laws lies in their suitability to the particular conditions that obtain in each nation. Therefore every nation must have its own form of government. However, public policy in all nations should require toleration in religious and intellectual matters as a guarantee of peace and freedom. Montesquieu was an innovator in political theory whose influence is still felt today.

The following selections are from The Persian Letters *(N.Y., Meridian Books, 1961), and the Nugent translation of* The Spirit of the Laws *(N.Y., Hafner Publishing Company, 1949).*

SOURCE. Montesquieu, *The Persian Letters,* translated by J. Robert Loy. Copyright © 1961 by Meridian Books, Inc. Reprinted by permission of the World Publishing Company.

THE PERSIAN LETTERS

Letter XXIV

Rica to Ibben in Smyrna. We have been in Paris for a month and have been continually in motion. It takes much doing to find a place to live, to meet people to whom you are recommended, and to provide yourself with necessities all at the same time.

Paris is as large as Ispahan. The houses here are so high that you would swear they were all inhabited by astrologers. You can readily understand that a city built up in the air, with six or seven houses built one on top of the other, is an extremely populous city, and that when everyone is down in the streets, there is great confusion.

Perhaps you will not believe this, but for the month I have been here, I have seen nobody walking. There are no people in the world who get so much out of their carcasses as the French: they run; they fly. The slow carriages of Asia, the regular pace of our camels, would make them swoon. As for myself, I am not built that way, and when I go walking, as I do often, without changing my pace, I sometimes fume and rage like a Christian. For, passing over the fact that I am splashed from head to foot, still I cannot forgive the elbowings in my ribs that I collect regularly and periodically. A man walking behind me, passes me and turns me half-around; then another, coming toward me from the opposite direction, briskly puts me back into the position where the first fellow hit me. I have barely made a hundred paces before I am more bruised than if I had gone ten leagues.

Do not expect me to be able just now to talk to you seriously about European usages and customs. I have only a faint idea of them myself and have barely had time to be amazed by them.

The King of France[1] is the most powerful prince of Europe. Unlike his neighbor the King of Spain, he has no gold mines. Yet he possesses greater riches, for he draws from the vanity of his subjects a wealth more inexhaustible than mines. He has been known to undertake and wage great wars with no other funds than honorary titles to sell, and by reason of this miracle of human pride, his troops are paid, his fortresses armed, and his navies fitted out.

Moreover, this king is a great magician. He exercises his empire

[1] [Louis XIV.]

over the very minds of his subjects and makes them think as he likes. If he has only one million crowns in his treasury and he needs two million, he has only to convince them that one crown equals two, and they believe him. If he is involved in a war that is difficult in the waging and finds himself short of money, he has only to put into their heads the notion that a slip of paper is money, and they are immediately convinced. He even goes so far as to make them believe that he can cure them of all manner of disease by touching them, so great is his strength and dominion over their minds.

What I am telling you about this prince ought not astonish you. For there is another magician even more powerful than the first and who has no less dominion over the mind of the first than that one has over the minds of others. This magician is called the Pope. Sometimes he has the King believing that three are only one, sometimes that the bread he eats is not bread and the wine he drinks not wine, and a thousand other things of the sort. . . .

Letter XXIX

Rica to Ibben in Smyrna. The Pope is the head of the Christians. He is an old idol worshipped out of habit. Formerly he was to be feared even by kings, for he deposed them as easily as our magnificent sultans depose the kings of Imirette and Georgia. But now he is no longer feared. He claims that he is the successor of one of the first Christians, who is called Saint Peter, and his is most certainly a rich succession, for he has immense treasures and a great country under his domination.

Bishops are lawyers subordinate to him, and they have, under his authority, two quite different functions. When they are assembled together they create, as does he, articles of faith. When they are acting individually they have scarcely any other function except to give dispensation from fulfilling the law. For you must know that the Christian religion is weighed down with an infinity of very difficult practices. And since it has been decided that it is less easy to fulfill these duties than to have bishops around who can dispense with them, this last alternative was chosen out of a sense of common good. In this way, if you don't wish to keep Ramadan,[2] if you don't choose to be subjected to the formalities

2 [I.e., Lent.]

of marriage, if you wish to break your vows, if you would like to marry in contravention of the prohibitions of the law, even sometimes if you want to break a sworn oath—you go to the bishop or the Pope and you are given immediate dispensation.

Bishops do not create articles of faith by their own decision. There are countless doctors, most of them dervishes,[3] who introduce among themselves thousands of new questions touching upon religion. They are allowed to dispute at great length, and the war goes on until a decision comes along to finish it.

And thus I can assure you that there never has been a kingdom where there are so many civil wars as in the Kingdom of Christ. . . .

Letter XLVI

Usbek to Rhedi in Venice. I keep seeing here people who argue endlessly about religion. But at the same time, they seem to be vying with each other as to who shall observe it the least.

They are not only not better Christians, but also not even better citizens, and that's what touches me, for under whatever religion one lives, the observance of laws, love for fellow men, and piety toward one's parents are always the first acts of religion.

In truth, should not the first object of a religious man be to please the divinity who established the religion he professes? The best means of succeeding in this is doubtless to observe the rules of society and the duties of humanity. For under whatever religion a man lives, from the moment that a supposition of religion exists, there must also be the supposition that God loves men, since he established a religion to make them happy, and since if he loves men, men are thus assured of pleasing him by also loving them, that is, by practicing all the duties of charity and human kindness in their behalf and never violating the laws under which they live.

So doing, we are much surer of pleasing God than we are by observing such and such a ceremony. For ceremonies contain no degree of goodness in themselves. They are good only with reference to and in the supposition of the knowledge that God has commanded them. But there is matter here for a long discussion. One can easily be deceived, since he must choose the ceremonies of one religion as over against two thousand. . . .

---

[3] [Applied by Montesquieu's Persians to the friars, especially to the Jesuits.]

Letter LIX

Rica to Usbek in ———. . . . It seems to me, Usbek, that we never judge of matters except by a secret reflex we make upon ourselves. I am not surprised that Negroes should paint the devil in blinding white, and their own gods black as coal; nor that the Venus of certain tribes should have paps hanging to her knees; nor that all idolaters should have pictured their gods with human faces, and should have advised them of all their own inclinations. It has been well said that if triangles were to create a god, they would give him three sides.

My dear Usbek, when I see men crawling about on an atom, I mean the earth, which is only a speck of the universe, and proposing themselves as models of divine providence, I don't know how to reconcile so much extravagance with so much pettiness.

From Paris, the 14th of the
Moon of Saphar, 1714.

Letter LXIX

Usbek to Rhedi in Venice. You could never have imagined that I should turn more metaphysician than I already was. And yet that's what has happened; you will be convinced of it once you have endured this outburst of my philosophy.

The most reasonable philosophers who have reflected on the nature of God have held that he is a being completely perfect, but they have sorely abused that idea. They have made an enumeration of all the different perfections that man is capable of having or imagining and have weighed down their notion of the divinity with them, without reflecting that often these attributes are mutually restrictive and that they cannot exist in the same being without destroying one another.

Poets of the West say that a painter who wanted to make the portrait of the goddess of beauty assembled the most beautiful Greek women and took from each her most pleasing feature, from which he reconstituted an entity that he believed to resemble the most beautiful of all the goddesses. If a man had tried to conclude from this that she was blonde as well as brunette and that she had both black eyes and blue eyes, that she was haughty as well as tender, he would have been taken for a fool.

Often God is lacking in one perfection that would be capable of endowing him with a great imperfection. But he is never limited save by himself. He is his own necessity. Thus, although God is omnipotent, he cannot break his promises nor can he deceive mankind. Often the impotence is most likely to be not in him, but in related things, and that is why he cannot change the essence of things.

. . .

Do not, however, for one moment believe that I am trying to limit the knowledge of God. Since he causes his creatures to move at his fancy, he knows all he wants to know. But even though he can see everything, he does not always use this faculty. Normally he leaves to his creature the faculty of acting or not acting, in order to leave to the creature the possibility of merit or demerit. It is then that he gives up his right of acting upon the creature or determining that action. But when he wants to know something, he knows it from all time, for he has only to will that it happen as he sees it and to determine his creatures in conformity with his will. Thus it is that he draws forth what is to happen from the number of purely possible things by fixing with his decree the future determinations of minds and by depriving them of the power he has granted them either to act or not to act.

. . .

My dear Rhedi, why so much philosophy? God is so sublime that we cannot even perceive his clouds. We know him well only through his precepts. He is immense, spiritual, infinite. May his grandeur bring us back to a realization of our weakness. Always humiliating the self means adoring him always.

From Paris, the last of the
Moon of Shahban, 1714.

Letter LXXV

Usbek to Rhedi in Venice. I must confess that I have not noticed in Christians that lively conviction of religion which obtains among the Mohammedans. There is much distance with them between profession of faith and belief, between belief and conviction, and between conviction and practice. Religion is less a matter of holiness than an excuse for dispute, open to everyone.

Courtiers, warriors, even women, rise up against ecclesiastics and demand that the churchmen prove what they are resolved never to believe. It's not a question of their being determined by reason nor is it a case of their having taken the trouble to examine the truth or falsehood of the religion they reject: these are rebels who have felt the yoke and shake it off before getting to know it. Thus they are no more certain of their disbelief than they are of their belief. . . .

A long time ago Christian princes freed all their slaves from servitude because, they said, Christianity makes all men equal. It is true that this act of religion was very useful to them: they thereby humbled the great lords, from whose power they retrieved the common masses. Subsequently, they made conquests in countries where they saw it was to their advantage to have slaves; they allowed the buying and selling of them, oblivious of the principle of their religion which had so touched them. How shall I put it? Truth in one era, falsehood in another. Why do we not do as the Christians! We are quite simple-minded to refuse business establishments and easy conquests in benign climates only because the water there is not sufficiently pure to allow us to wash according to the principles of the holy Koran!

I render thanks unto the all-powerful God, who sent Ali, his great prophet, that I profess a religion that comes first before all human concerns, and that is as pure as the heaven from which it descended.

> From Paris, the 13th of the
> Moon of Saphar, 1715.

Letter LXXXIII

Usbek to Rhedi in Venice. If there is a God, Rhedi, of necessity he must be just, for if he were not, he would be the most evil and imperfect of all beings.

Justice is a true relationship of appropriateness which exists between two things, and this relationship is always the same, no matter by whom considered, whether it be God, or an angel, or finally, a man.

It is true that men do not always see these relationships. Often even, when they do see them, they draw away from them; their own profit is always what they see most clearly. Justice raises her voice, but she has trouble being heard amid the tumult of passions.

Men are capable of doing injustice because it is to their own interest to do so, and because they prefer their own satisfaction to that of others. It is always by reference to themselves that they act; no man is evil gratuitously. There must be some determinant reason; that reason is always a selfish one.

But it is not possible that God should ever do anything unjust. By the very fact that we can suppose he sees justice, he must necessarily follow it, for since he needs nothing and is sufficient unto himself, he would otherwise be the most wicked of all beings, for he would be so with no incentive.

Thus, even were there to be no God, we should always love justice—that is to say, do our best to resemble that being of whom we have such a beautiful idea, who if he were to exist, would be, of necessity, just. Free though we might be from the yoke of religion, we ought never to be free from that of equity.

That, Rhedi, is what made me think that justice is eternal and not dependent on the conventions of men. If it should so depend, this would be a horrible truth that we should have to hide from ourselves.

.   .   .

From Paris, the 1st of the
Moon of Gemmadi I, 1715.

Letter LXXXV

Usbek to Mirza in Ispahan. You know, Mirza, that some of Shah Suleiman's ministers had formed the plan of forcing all Armenians in Persia to leave the realm or become Mohammedans, with the idea in mind that our empire would always be polluted as long as it kept the heathen in our midst.

Persian greatness would have come to an end if blind religious devotion had had its way on that occasion.

It is not known why the project failed: neither those who proposed it nor those who rejected it ever knew the train of events. Chance fulfilled the office of reason and policy, and saved the empire from a greater peril than it would have been exposed to by the loss of a battle and the capture of two cities.

By proscribing the Armenians, they were within an ace of destroying, in one single day, all the businessmen and almost all the artisans of the realm. I am sure that the great Shah Abbas would rather have had both arms cut off than have signed such an order, and that he would have considered sending his most industrious subjects to the Mogul and other kings of the Indies tantamount to giving them half of his states.

The persecutions made by our zealous Mohammedans at the expense of the Ghebers forced the latter to migrate en masse to the Indies, and thus deprived Persia of that people so diligent in husbandry that, by itself, it was in a position to conquer the sterility of our soil.

There remained only this second attempt for religious devotion to fall back on: that is, to destroy industry, in consequence of which the empire would have fallen apart of its own accord, and along with it, of necessity, the very religion that the zealots wanted to make so flourishing.

If I must reason straightforwardly, Mirza, I'm not sure that it wouldn't be a good thing for a state to have several religions.

.   .   .

From Paris, the 26th of the
Moon of Gemmadi I, 1715.

Letter XCVII

Usbek to Hassein, Dervish of the Mountain of Jaron. O thou, wise dervish, whose inquiring mind sparkles with such great knowledge, hear what I am about to tell thee.

There exist here philosophers who, in truth, have not yet attained to the zenith of Oriental wisdom. They have not yet been transported in rapture to the luminous throne. They have neither heard the ineffable words that resound throughout the concerts of angels, nor felt the fearful manifestation of divine frenzy. Rather, left to themselves, deprived of holy miracles, they are following silently the paths of human reason.

Thou couldst not possibly believe how far this guide has taken them. They have untangled chaos and have explained, by simple mechanics, the order of divine architecture. The author of nature gave movement to matter; no more was necessary to produce this prodigious variety of effects which we see in the universe.

Let ordinary lawmakers propose to us laws 'for regulating human societies—laws as subject to change as the minds of those who proposed them and those who observe them. These other thinkers speak only of general laws, immutable, eternal, which are to be observed without exception, with an order, a regularity, and infinite immediacy in the immensity of space.

Now what, O holy man, dost thou think these laws are? Thou mayest perhaps imagine that entering here into the council of the Eternal, thou shalt be astonished by the sublimity of mysteries. Thou givest up any pretension to understand in advance; thou art prepared only to admire.

But thou must soon change thy thinking. These laws do not blind with false respect; their simplicity has kept them unknown for a long time, and it is only after much reflection that all the depth and extent of them has been comprehended.

The first law is that every body tends to move in a straight line unless it meets some obstacle that deflects it. The second, which is but a natural consequence, is that every body that revolves about a center point tends to withdraw from the center, for the farther away it is, the more the line it describes approaches a straight line.

Therein, O sublime dervish, lies the key of nature; these are pregnant principles from which flow endless consequences. . . .

Letter CV

Rhedi to Usbek in Paris. You have spoken much, in one of your letters, about the arts and sciences cultivated in the West. You will consider me a barbarian, but I am not so sure that the profit drawn from them can make reparation to men for the bad use made of them daily.

I have heard it said that the invention of mortar shells in itself deprived all the peoples of Europe of their freedom. Princes, no longer able to entrust the protection of fortified cities to burghers, who would have surrendered at the first shelling, have therefore had an excuse for maintaining great bodies of regular troops, with which, subsequently, they have oppressed their subjects.

You know that since the invention of gunpowder, there is no impregnable city, which is to say, Usbek, that there is no asylum on earth against violence and unjustice.

I am ever trembling lest someone should fall upon some secret that makes possible a shortened path to the destruction of men, peoples, and entire nations. . . .

Happy ignorance of Mohammed's children! Lovable simplicity, so cherished by our Holy Prophet, you recall to me always the innocence of olden times and the peace that ruled in the hearts of our forefathers.

From Venice, the 2nd of the
Moon of Ramadan, 1717.

Letter CXXII

Usbek to the Same. Mildness of government contributes in a marvelous way to the propagation of the species. All republics are a constant proof of this, and more than all the others, Switzerland and Holland, which is to say the worst countries in Europe if the nature of the terrain is taken into consideration. Yet they are the most populous.

Nothing will attract foreigners more than freedom and the abundance that always follows from it. The first is sought after for itself, and we are led by our needs to seek out the country where the other is found.

The human race multiplies in a country where abundance furnishes all the needs of children without in any way diminishing the subsistence of their fathers.

The very equality of citizens, which ordinarily produces equality of fortune, brings abundance and life into every organ of the body politic and extends such benefits generally.

The same cannot be said of countries subjected to arbitrary power: the prince, the courtiers, and a few individuals possess all the wealth, while the others moan in extreme poverty.

If a man is not well off and feels that he will produce children even poorer than himself, he will not marry; if he marries, he will be afraid of having too many children, who might finish off the paternal fortune and thus drop lower than their father's status. . . .

Letter CXXV

Rica to ———. For every religion, there has always existed the embarrassing problem of giving some idea of the pleasures awaiting those who have lived well. One can easily terrify the wicked with a long list of threatened punishments. But as for the virtuous, it is not easy to know what to promise them. It seems that it is of the very nature of pleasures to be of short duration; imagination finds it difficult to picture any others.

I have seen descriptions of paradise capable of making all sensible people give it up. Some have the happy shades playing a flute eternally; others condemn them to taking strolls forever; still others, who have them dreaming up there of their mistresses here below, have not realized that a hundred million years constitute a sufficiently long time to remove the taste for such amorous concerns. . . .

Letter CXLV

Usbek to —————— . . . In time past all scholars were accused of black magic. I am not a bit surprised by this. Each man would say to himself: "I have developed my natural talents of study as far as they can go. And yet a certain scholar holds advantages over me; therefore, there must be something diabolic in this business."

Now that such accusations have fallen into discredit, another tack has been taken, and a scholar can scarcely avoid the reproach of irreligion or heresy. It does him no good to be absolved by the people; the wound is still there and will never close. For him this will always be a sore spot. An adversary will come along thirty years after and say modestly: "God forbid I should say that what you are accused of is true, but you *were* obliged to justify yourself." And thus a scholar's very justification is turned against him.

If he writes some story and is noble in mind and upright in heart, people will think up a thousand persecutions. They will go arouse the magistrate against him about an event that happened a thousand years ago. They will require that his pen be captive if it refuses to be venal.

Happier are those cowardly men who abandon their faith for a mediocre annuity, who if you took all their impostures one by one, would be selling them at less than an obol each, who overthrow the constitution of the empire, lessen the rights of one power and increase those of another—giving to princes, taking away from the people, resuscitating superannuated laws, flattering the passions that are in style in their era, and the vices that exist on the throne, imposing all the more unworthily on posterity as posterity has less and less means for destroying their testimony.

But it is not enough for an author to have suffered all these insults, not enough for him to have remained in continued uneasiness over the success of his work. Finally, that work, which has cost him so much effort, sees the light of day. It draws quarrels down upon his head from every quarter. And how can he avoid them? He had a certain feeling on a matter; he upheld it in his writings. Little did he know that a man two hundred leagues away had said exactly the opposite. Nevertheless, here begins the declaration of war.

If only, at least, he could hope to receive some little consideration! No. At best, he can hope for some esteem only from those who are devoted to the same branch of science as he. A philosopher holds sovereign scorn for a man whose head is loaded with facts. He is himself considered a dreamer by the man who has a good memory.

As to those who proudly profess their ignorance, they would like the whole human race to be buried in that oblivion in which they themselves will be buried. . . .

From Paris, the 26th of the
Moon of Shahban, 1720.

THE SPIRIT OF THE LAWS

Preface

I have first of all considered mankind, and the result of my thoughts has been that amidst such an infinite diversity of laws and manners, they were not solely conducted by the caprice of fancy.

I have laid down the first principles, and have found that the particular cases follow naturally from them; that the histories of all nations are only consequences of them; and that every partic-

SOURCE. Montesquieu, *The Spirit of the Laws*, Nugent translation. Reprinted with permission of Hafner, 1949.

ular law is connected with another law, or depends on some other
of a more general extent. . . .

I have not drawn my principles from my prejudices, but from
the nature of things.

Here a great many truths will not appear till we have seen the
chain which connects them with others. The more we enter into
particulars, the more we shall perceive the certainty of the principles on which they are founded. I have not even given all these
particulars, for who could mention them all without a most
insupportable fatigue?

Book I

Of Laws in General

1. Of the Relation of Laws to Different Beings

Laws, in their most general signification, are the necessary
relations arising from the nature of things. In this sense all beings
have their laws: the Deity His laws, the material world its laws,
the intelligences superior to man their laws, the beasts their laws,
man his laws.

They who assert that a blind fatality produced the various
effects we behold in this world talk very absurdly; for can anything be more unreasonable than to pretend that a blind fatality
could be productive of intelligent beings?

There is, then, a prime reason; and laws are the relations subsisting between it and different beings, and the relations of these
to one another.

God is related to the universe, as Creator and Preserver; the
laws by which He created all things are those by which He
preserves them. He acts according to these rules, because He knows
them; He knows them, because He made them; and He made
them; because they are in relation of His wisdom and power.

Since we observe that the world, though formed by the motion
of matter, and void of understanding, subsists through so long a
succession of ages, its motions must certainly be directed by
invariable laws; and could we imagine another world, it must also
have constant rules, or it would inevitably perish.

Thus the creation, which seems an arbitrary act, supposes laws
as invariable as those of the fatality of the atheists. It would be
absurd to say that the Creator might govern the world without
these rules, since without them it could not subsist.

These rules are a fixed and invariable relation. In bodies moved, the motion is received, increased, diminished, or lost according to the relations of the quantity of matter and velocity; each diversity is uniformity, each change is constancy.

Particular intelligent beings may have laws of their own making, but they have some likewise which they never made. Before there were intelligent beings, they were possible; they had, therefore, possible relations, and consequently, possible laws. Before laws were made, there were relations of possible justice. To say that there is nothing just or unjust but what is commanded or forbidden by positive laws is the same as saying that before the describing of a circle all the radii were not equal.

We must therefore acknowledge relations of justice antecedent to the positive law by which they are established: as, for instance, if human societies existed, it would be right to conform to their laws; if there were intelligent beings that had received a benefit of another being, they ought to show their gratitude; if one intelligent being had created another intelligent being, the latter ought to continue in its original state of dependence; if one intelligent being injures another, it deserves a retaliation; and so on. . . .

3. Of Positive Laws

As soon as man enters into a state of society he loses the sense of his weakness; equality ceases, and then commences the state of war.

Each particular society begins to feel its strength, whence arises a state of war between different nations. The individuals likewise of each society become sensible of their force; hence the principal advantages of this society they endeavor to convert to their own emolument, which constitutes a state of war between individuals.

These two different kinds of states give rise to human laws. Considered as inhabitants of so great a planet, which necessarily contains a variety of nations, they have laws relating to their mutual intercourse, which is what we call the law of nations. As members of a society that must be properly supported, they have laws relating to the governors and the governed, and this we distinguish by the name of political law. They have also another sort of laws, as they stand in relation to each other; by which is understood the civil law. . . .

Law in general is human reason, inasmuch as it governs all the inhabitants of the earth: the political and civil laws of each nation ought to be only the particular cases in which human reason is applied.

They should be adapted in such a manner to the people for whom they are framed that it should be a great chance if those of one nation suit another.

They should be in relation to the nature and principle of each government: whether they form it, as may be said of political laws; or whether they support it, as in the case of civil institutions.

They should be in relation to the climate of each country, to the quality of its soil, to its situation and extent, to the principal occupation of the natives, whether husbandmen, huntsmen, or shepherds; they should have relation to the degree of liberty which the constitution will bear; to the religion of the inhabitants, to their inclinations, riches, numbers, commerce, manners, and customs. In fine, they have relations to each other, as also to their origin, to the intent of the legislator, and to the order of things on which they are established; in all of which different lights they ought to be considered.

This is what I have undertaken to perform in the following work. These relations I shall examine, since all these together constitute what I call the Spirit of Laws.

I have not separated the political from the civil institutions, as I do not pretend to treat of laws, but of their spirit; and as this spirit consists in the various relations which the laws may bear to different objects, it is not so much my business to follow the natural order of laws as that of these relations and objects.

I shall first examine the relations which laws bear to the nature and principle of each government; and as this principle has a strong influence on laws, I shall make it my study to understand it thoroughly: and if I can but once establish it, the laws will soon appear to flow thence as from their source. I shall proceed afterward to other and more particular relations.

Book II

Of Laws Directly Derived from the Nature of Government

1. Of the Nature of Three Different Governments

There are three species of government: republican, monarchical, and despotic. In order to discover their nature, it is sufficient to recollect the common notion which supposes three definitions, or rather three facts: that a republican government is that in which the body, or only a part of the people, is possessed of the supreme power; monarchy, that in which a single person governs by fixed and established laws; a despotic government, that in which a single person directs everything by his own will and caprice.

This is what I call the nature of each government; we must now inquire into those laws which directly conform to this nature, and consequently are the fundamental institutions. . . .

Book III

Of the Principles of the Three Kinds of Government

9. Of the Principle of Despotic Government

As virtue is necessary in a republic, and in a monarchy honor, so fear is necessary in a despotic government: with regard to virtue, there is no occasion for it, and honor would be extremely dangerous. . . .

11. Reflections on the Preceding Chapters

Such are the principles of the three sorts of government: which does not imply that in a particular republic they actually are, but that they ought to be, virtuous; nor does it prove that in a particular monarchy they are actuated by honor, or in a particular despotic government by fear; but that they ought to be directed by these principles, otherwise the government is imperfect.

Book V

That the Laws Given by the Legislator Ought To Be in Relation to the Principle of Government

1. Idea of This Book

That the laws of education should relate to the principle of each government has been shown in the preceding book. Now the same may be said of those which the legislator gives to the whole society. The relation of laws to this principle strengthens the several springs of government; and this principle derives thence, in its turn, a new degree of vigor. And thus it is in mechanics that action is always followed by reaction.

Our design is to examine this relation to each government, beginning with the republican state, the principle of which is virtue.

2. *What Is Meant by Virtue in a Political State*

. . . The love of our country is conducive to a purity of morals, and the latter is again conducive to the former. The less we are able to satisfy our private passions, the more we abandon ourselves to those of a general nature. How comes it that monks are so fond of their order? It is owing to the very cause that renders the order insupportable. Their rule debars them from all those things by which the ordinary passions are fed; there remains therefore only this passion for the very rule that torments them. The more austere it is, that is, the more it curbs their inclinations, the more force it gives to the only passion left them. . . .

3. *What Is Meant by a Love of the Republic in a Democracy*

A love of the republic in a democracy is a love of the democracy; as the latter is that of equality.

A love of the democracy is likewise that of frugality. Since every individual ought here to enjoy the same happiness and the same advantages, they should consequently taste the same pleasures and form the same hopes, which cannot be expected but from a general frugality. . . .

Book VIII

Of the Corruption of the Principles of the Three Governments

1. *General Idea of This Book*

The corruption of every government generally begins with that of its principles.

2. *Of the Corruption of the Principles of Democracy*

The principles of democracy are corrupted not only when the spirit of equality is extinct, but likewise when they fall into a spirit of extreme equality, and when each citizen would fain be upon a level with those whom he has chosen to command him. Then the people, incapable of bearing the very power they have delegated, want to manage everything themselves, to debate for the senate, to execute for the magistrate, and to decide for the judges.

When this is the case, virtue can no longer subsist in the republic. The people are desirous of exercising the functions of the magistrates, who cease to be revered. The deliberations of the senate are slighted; all respect is then laid aside for the senators, and consequently for old age. If there is no more respect for old age, there will be none presently for parents; deference to husbands will be likewise thrown off, and submission to masters. This license will soon become general, and the trouble of command be as fatiguing as that of obedience. Wives, children, slaves, will shake off all subjection. No longer will there by any such thing as manners, order, or virtue. . . .

16. Distinctive Properties of a Republic

It is natural for a republic to have only a small territory; otherwise it cannot long subsist. In an extensive republic there are men of large fortunes, and consequently of less moderation; there are trusts too considerable to be placed in any single subject; he has interests of his own; he soon begins to think that he may be happy and glorious by oppressing his fellow citizens; and that he may raise himself to grandeur on the ruins of his country.

Book XI

Of the Laws Which Establish Political Liberty with Regard to the Constitution

1. A General Idea

I make a distinction between the laws that establish political liberty as it relates to the constitution, and those by which it is established as it relates to the citizen. The former shall be the subject of this book; the latter I shall examine in the next.

2. Different Significations of the Word "Liberty"

There is no word that admits of more various significations, and has made more varied impressions on the human mind, than that of "liberty." Some have taken it as a means of deposing a person on whom they had conferred a tyrannical authority; others for the power of choosing a superior whom they are obliged to obey; others for the right of bearing arms, and of being thereby enabled to use violence; others, in fine, for the privilege of being governed by a native of their own country, or by their own laws.

A certain nation for a long time thought liberty consisted in the privilege of wearing a long beard. Some have annexed this name to one form of government exclusive of others: those who had a republican taste applied it to this species of polity; those who liked a monarchical state gave it to monarchy. Thus they have all applied the name of liberty to the government most suitable to their own customs and inclinations: and as in republics the people have not so constant and so present a view of the causes of their misery, and as the magistrates seem to act only in conformity to the laws, hence liberty is generally said to reside in republics, and to be banished from monarchies. In fine, as in democracies the people seem to act almost as they please, this sort of government has been deemed the most free, and the power of the people has been confounded with their liberty.

3. *In What Liberty Consists*

It is true that in democracies the people seem to act as they please; but political liberty does not consist in an unlimited freedom. In governments, that is, in societies directed by laws, liberty can consist only in the power of doing what we ought to will, and in not being constrained to do what we ought not to will.

We must continually present to our minds the difference between independence and liberty. Liberty is a right of doing whatever the laws permit, and if a citizen could do what they forbid, he would be no longer possessed of liberty, because all his fellow citizens would have the same power.

4. *The Same Subject Continued*

Democratic and aristocratic states are not in their own nature free. Political liberty is to be found only in moderate governments; and even in these it is not always found. It is there only when there is no abuse of power. But constant experience shows us that every man invested with power is apt to abuse it, and to carry his authority as far as it will go. Is it not strange, though true, to say that virtue itself has need of limits?

To prevent this abuse, it is necessary from the very nature of things that power should be a check to power. A government may be so constituted as no man shall be compelled to do things to which the law does not oblige him, nor forced to abstain from things which the law permits. . . .

6. *Of the Constitution of England*

. . . The political liberty of the subject is a tranquillity of mind arising from the opinion each person has of his safety. In order to have this liberty, it is requisite the government be so constituted as one man need not be afraid of another.

When the legislative and executive powers are united in the same person, or in the same body of magistrates, there can be no liberty, because apprehensions may arise lest the same monarch or senate should enact tyrannical laws to execute them in a tyrannical manner.

Again, there is no liberty if the judiciary power be not separated from the legislative; the life and liberty of the subject would be exposed to arbitrary control, for the judge would then be the legislator. Were it joined to the executive power, the judge might behave with violence and oppression.

There would be an end of everything were the same man or the same body, whether of the nobles or of the people, to exercise those three powers, that of enacting laws, that of executing the public resolutions, and of trying the causes of individuals.

Book XII

Of the Laws That Form Political Liberty,
in Relation to the Subject

1. *Idea of This Book*

It is not sufficient to have treated political liberty in relation to the constitution, we must examine it likewise in the relation it bears to the subject.

We have observed that in the former case it arises from a certain distribution of the three powers; but in the latter, we must consider it in another light. It consists in security, or in the opinion people have of their security. . . .

5. *Of Certain Accusations That Require Particular Moderation and Prudence*

It is an important maxim that we ought to be very circumspect in the prosecution of witchcraft and heresy. The accusation of these two crimes may be vastly injurious to liberty, and productive of infinite oppression, if the legislator knows not how to set bounds to it. For as it does not directly point at a person's actions, but at his character, it grows dangerous in proportion to the ignorance of the people; and then a man is sure to be always in danger, because the most exceptional conduct, the purest morals, and the constant practice of every duty in life are not a sufficient security against the suspicion of his being guilty of the like crimes. . . .

12. Of Indiscreet Speeches

. . . Words do not constitute an overt act; they remain only in idea. When considered by themselves, they have generally no determinate signification, for this depends on the tone in which they are uttered. It often happens that in repeating the same words they have not the same meaning; this depends on their connection with other things, and sometimes more is signified by silence than by any expression whatever. Since there can be nothing so equivocal and ambiguous as all this, how is it possible to convert it into a crime of high treason? Wherever this law is established, there is an end not only of liberty, but even of its very shadow.

Book XVII

*How the Laws of Political Servitude Bear a Relation
to the Nature of Climate*

1. Of Political Servitude

Political servitude does not less depend on the nature of the climate than that which is civil and domestic; and this we shall now demonstrate.

2. The Difference Between Nations in Point of Courage

We have already observed that great heat enervates the strength and courage of men, and that in cold climates they have a certain vigor of body and mind, which renders them patient and intrepid, and qualifies them for arduous enterprises. This remark holds good not only between different nations but even in the different parts of the same country. . . .

We ought not, then, to be astonished that the effeminacy of the people in hot climates has almost always rendered them slaves; and that the bravery of those in cold climates has enabled them to maintain their liberties. This is an effect which springs from a natural cause.

This has been found true in America; the despotic empires of Mexico and Peru were near the line, and almost all the little free nations were, and are still, near the poles.

Book XIX

Of Laws in Relation to the Principles Which Form the General Spirit, the Morals, and Customs of a Nation

4. *Of the General Spirit of Mankind*

Mankind are influenced by various causes: by the climate, by the religion, by the laws, by the maxims of government, by precedents, morals, and customs; whence if formed a general spirit of nations. . . .

5. *How Far We Should Be Attentive Lest the General Spirit of a Nation Be Changed*

. . . It is the business of the legislature to follow the spirit of the nation, when it is not contrary to the principles of government; for we do nothing so well as when we act with freedom, and follow the bent of our natural genius.

If an air of pedantry be given to a nation that is naturally gay, the state will gain no advantage from it, either at home or abroad. Leave it to do the frivolous things in the most serious manner, and with gaiety the things most serious. . . .

14. *What Are the Natural Means of Changing the Manners and Customs of a Nation*

We have said that the laws were the particular and precise institutions of a legislator, and manners and customs the institutions of a nation in general. Hence it follows that when these manners and customs are to be changed, it ought not to be done by laws; this would have too much the air of tyranny: it would be better to change them by introducing other manners and other customs.

Thus when a prince would make great alterations in his kingdom, he should reform by law what is established by law, and change by custom what is settled by custom; for it is very bad policy to change by law what ought to be changed by custom. . . .

27. *How the Laws Contribute to Form the Manners, Customs, and Character of a Nation*

The customs of an enslaved people are a part of their servitude, those of a free people are a part of their liberty.

I have spoken in the eleventh book of a free people, and have given the principles of their constitution: let us now see the effects which follow from this liberty, the character it is capable of forming, and the customs which naturally result from it.

I do not deny that the climate may have produced a great part of the laws, manners, and customs of this nation; but I maintain that its manners and customs have a close connection with its laws.

As there are in this state two visible powers—the legislative and executive—and as every citizen has a will of his own, and may at pleasure assert his independence, most men have a greater fondness for one of these powers than for the other, and the multitude have commonly neither equity nor sense enough to show an equal affection to both. . . .

As the enjoyment of liberty, and even its support and preservation, consist in every man's being allowed to speak his thoughts, and to lay open his sentiments, a citizen in this state will say or write whatever the laws do not expressly forbid to be said or written.

A people like this, being always in a ferment, are more easily conducted by their passions than by reason, which never produces any great effect in the mind of man; it is therefore easy for those who govern to make them undertake enterprises contrary to their true interest. . . .

Book XXVI

Of Laws in Relation to the Order of Things Which They Determine

1. *Idea of This Book*

Men are governed by several kinds of laws: by the law of nature; by the divine law, which is that of religion; by ecclesiastical, otherwise called canon law, which is that of religious polity; by the law of nations, which may be considered as the civil law of the whole globe, in which sense every nation is a citizen; by the general political law, which relates to that human wisdom whence all societies derive their origin; by the particular political law, the object of which is each society; by the law of conquest founded on this, that one nation has been willing and able, or has had a right, to offer violence to another; by the civil law of every society, by which a citizen may defend his possessions and his life against the attacks of any other citizen; in fine, by domestic law, which proceeds from a society's being divided into several families, all of which have need of a particular government.

There are therefore different orders of laws, and the sublimity of human reason consists in perfectly knowing to which of these orders the things that are to be determined ought to have a principal relation, and not to throw into confusion those principles which should govern mankind.

2. Of Laws Divine and Human

We ought not to decide by divine laws what should be decided by human laws; nor determine by human what should be determined by divine laws.

These two sorts of laws differ in their origin, in their object, and in their nature.

2 *Voltaire*

François Marie Arouet, self-titled de Voltaire, embarked on a literary career that very soon occasioned his flight to England. The result was the Letters on the English *(1733) that made his reputation as a philosopher. In 1750 Voltaire went to Berlin where for three years he worked on* The Philosophical Dictionary, *till his quarrels with Frederick II of Prussia caused him to flee once more.* The Philosophical Dictionary *is representative of Voltaire's large body of work which may be grouped under three headings: science, religion, and social theory.*

Locke and Newton's scientific epistemology provided Voltaire with a theoretical basis for his natural religion. Voltaire main-

SOURCE. From *The Works of Voltaire,* translated by William F. Fleming, 24 Vols., E.R. Du Mont, 1901.

*tained that God's attributes are unknown to men: therefore
everything is sectarian but the simple worship of God and the
practice of virtue. This religion is not a new invention, he declared, but is as old as mankind, and as natural and universal as
reason. Benevolence could only be practiced when all men were
united as brothers, through reason, in natural religion.*

*Voltaire defined good and evil with reference to social behavior,
but he traced the source of both to the individual himself. Man
like everything else in nature is just what he ought to be, the
point being not to define his nature but to change his social
behavior. Voltaire was primarily interested in reforming mankind
rather than in renovating human thought, although right acting,
he believed, grew out of right thinking. Hence the importance of
reason to man in his quest for freedom.*

PHILOSOPHICAL DICTIONARY

Adam

So much has been said and so much written concerning Adam,
his wife, and the pre-Adamites, etc., and the rabbis have put forth
so many idle stories respecting Adam, and it is so dull to repeat
what others have said before, that I shall here hazard an idea
entirely new; one, at least, which is not to be found in any ancient
author, father of the church, preacher, theologian, critic, or
scholar with whom I am acquainted. I mean the profound *secrecy*
with respect to Adam which was observed throughout the habitable earth, Palestine only excepted, until the time when the
Jewish books began to be known in Alexandria, and were translated into Greek under one of the Ptolemies. Still they were very
little known, for large books were very rare and very dear.
Besides, the Jews of Jerusalem were so incensed against those of
Alexandria, loaded them with so many reproaches for having
translated their Bible into a profane tongue, called them so many
ill names, and cried so loudly to the Lord, that the Alexandrian
Jews concealed their translation as much as possible; it was so
secret that no Greek or Roman author speaks of it before the
time of the Emperor Aurelian.

. . .

We do not see the name of *Noah* or of *Adam* in any of the ancient dynasties of Egypt: they are not to be found among the Chaldeans; in a word, the whole earth has been silent respecting them. It must be owned that such a silence is unparalleled. Every people has attributed to itself some imaginary origin, yet none has approached the true one. We cannot comprehend how the father of all nations has so long been unknown, while in the natural course of things his name should have been carried from mouth to mouth to the farthest corners of the earth.

Let us humble ourselves to the decrees of that Providence which has permitted so astonishing an oblivion. All was mysterious and concealed in the nation guided by God Himself, which prepared the way for Christianity, and was the wild olive on which the fruitful one has been grafted. That the names of the authors of mankind should be unknown to mankind is a mystery of the highest order.

The Beautiful

Ask a toad what is beauty—the great beauty, *to kalon;* he will answer that it is the female with two great round eyes coming out of her little head; her large flat mouth; her yellow belly and brown back. Ask a Negro of Guinea; beauty is to him a black, oily skin, sunken eyes, and a flat nose. Ask the devil; he will tell you that the beautiful consists in a pair of horns, four claws, and a tail. Then consult the philosophers; they will answer you with jargon; they must have something conformable to the archetype of the essence of the beautiful—to the *to kalon.*

. . .

There are actions which the whole world considers fine. . . .

A friend devotes himself to death for his friend; a son, for his father. The Algonquins, the French, the Chinese, will mutually say that all this is very beautiful, that such actions give them pleasure, and that they admire them.

They will say the same of great moral maxims; of that of Zoroaster: "If in doubt that an action be just, desist"; of that of Confucius: "Forget injuries; never forget benefits."

The Negro, with round eyes and flattened nose, who would not give the ladies of our court the name of beautiful, would give it without hesitation to these actions and these maxims. Even the wicked man recognizes the beauty of the virtues which he cannot imitate. The beautiful, which only strikes the senses, the imagination, and what is called the spirit, is then often uncertain; the beauty which strikes the heart is not. You will find a number of people who will tell you they have found nothing beautiful in three fourths of the *Iliad;* but nobody will deny that the devotion of Codrus for his people was fine, supposing it was true. . . .

Body

Body and matter are here the same thing, although there is hardly any such thing as synonym in the most rigorous sense of the word. There have been persons who by this word "body" have understood "spirit" also. They have said "spirit" originally signifies breath; only a body can breathe, therefore "body" and "spirit" may, after all, be the same thing. . . .

As we know not what a spirit is, so also we are ignorant of what a body is; we see various properties, but what is the subject in which those properties reside? "There is nothing but body," said Democritus and Epicurus; "there is no such thing as body," said the disciples of Zeno and Elea.

Berkeley, Bishop of Cloyne, is the last who, by a hundred captious sophisms, has pretended to prove that bodies do not exist. They have, says he, neither color, nor smell, nor heat; all these modalities are in your sensations, not in the objects. He might have spared himself the trouble of proving this truth, for it was already sufficiently known. But thence he passed to extent and solidity, which are essential to body, and thinks he proves that there is no extent in a piece of green cloth because the cloth is not in reality green, the sensation of green being in ourselves only, therefore the sensation of extent is likewise in ourselves only. Having thus destroyed extent he concludes that solidity, which is attached to it, falls of itself, and therefore that there is nothing in the world but our ideas. So that, according to this doctor, ten thousand men killed by ten thousand cannon shots are in reality nothing more than ten thousand apprehensions of our understanding, and when a female becomes pregnant it is only one idea lodged in another idea from which a third idea will be produced. . . .

We all resemble the greater part of the Parisian ladies who live well without knowing what is put in their ragouts; just so do we enjoy bodies without knowing of what they are composed. Of what does a body consist? Of parts, and these parts resolve themselves into other parts. What are these last parts? They, too, are bodies; you divide incessantly without making any progress. . . .

Climate

Influence of Climate. Climate influences religion in respect to ceremonies and usages. A legislator could have experienced no difficulty in inducing the Indians to bathe in the Ganges at certain appearances of the moon; it is a high gratification to them. Had anyone proposed a like bath to the people who inhabit the banks of the Dvina, near Archangel, he would have been stoned. Forbid pork to an Arab, who after eating this species of animal food (the most miserable and disgusting in his own country) would be affected by leprosy, he will obey you with joy; prohibit it to a Westphalian, and he will be tempted to knock you down. Abstinence from wine is a good precept of religion in Arabia, where orange, citron, and lemon waters are necessary to health. Mohammed would not have forbidden wine in Switzerland, especially before going to battle.

Religions have always turned on two pivots—forms and ceremonies, and faith. Forms and ceremonies depend much on climate; faith not at all. A doctrine will be received with equal facility under the equator or near the pole. It will be afterward equally rejected at Batavia and the Orcades, while it will be maintained, *unguibus et rostro*—with tooth and nail—at Salamanca. This depends not on sun and atmosphere, but solely upon opinion, that fickle empress of the world. . . .

Conscience

Of the Conscience of Good and of Evil. Locke has demonstrated —if we may use that term in morals and metaphysics—that we have no innate ideas or principles. He was obliged to demonstrate this position at great length, as the contrary was at that time universally believed. It hence clearly follows that it is necessary to instill just ideas and good principles into the mind as soon as it acquires the use of its faculties.

Locke adduces the example of savages, who kill and devour their neighbors without any remorse of conscience; and of Christian soldiers, decently educated, who, on the taking of a city by assault, plunder, slay, and violate, not merely without remorse, but with rapture, honor, and glory, and with the applause of all their comrades.

It is perfectly certain that, in the massacres of St. Bartholomew, and in the autos-da-fé, the holy acts of faith of the Inquisition, no murderer's conscience ever upbraided him with having massacred men, women, and children, or with the shrieks, faintings, and dying tortures of his miserable victims, whose only crime consisted in keeping Easter in a manner different from that of the inquisitors. It results, therefore, from what has been stated, that we have no other conscience than what is created in us by the spirit of the age, by example, and by our own dispositions and reflections.

Man is born without principles, but with the faculty of receiving them. His natural disposition will incline him either to cruelty or kindness; his understanding will in time inform him that the square of twelve is a hundred and forty-four, and that he ought not to do to others what he would not that others should do to him; but he will not, of himself, acquire these truths in early childhood. He will not understand the first, and he will not feel the second.

A young savage who, when hungry, has received from his father a piece of another savage to eat, will, on the morrow, ask for the like meal, without thinking about any obligation not to treat a neighbor otherwise than he would be treated himself. He acts, mechanically and irresistibly, directly contrary to the eternal principle.

Nature has made a provision against such horrors. She has given to man a disposition to pity, and the power of comprehending truth. These two gifts of God constitute the foundation of civil society. This is the reason there have ever been but few cannibals; and which renders life, among civilized nations, a little tolerable. Fathers and mothers bestow on their children an education which soon renders them social, and this education confers on them a conscience.

Country

A country is a composition of many families; and as a family is commonly supported on the principle of self-love, when, by an opposing interest, the same self-love extends to our town, our province, or our nation, it is called love of country. The greater a country becomes, the less we love it; for love is weakened by diffusion. It is impossible to love a family so numerous that all the members can scarcely be known.

. . .

It is lamentable that to be a good patriot we must become the enemy of the rest of mankind. That good citizen, the ancient Cato, always gave it as his opinion that Carthage must be destroyed: *Delenda est Carthago.* To be a good patriot is to wish our own country enriched by commerce, and powerful by arms; but such is the condition of mankind that to wish the greatness of our own country is often to wish evil to our neighbors. He who could bring himself to wish that his country should always remain as it is would be a citizen of the universe.

History

Of the Certainty of History. All certainty which does not consist in mathematical demonstration is nothing more than the highest probability; there is no other historical certainty.

When Marco Polo described the greatness and population of China, being the first, and for a time the only writer who had described them, he could not obtain credit. The Portuguese, who for ages afterward had communication and commerce with that vast empire, began to render the description probable. It is now a matter of absolute certainty; of that certainty which arises from unanimous deposition of a thousand witnesses of different nations, unopposed by the testimony of a single individual.

If merely two or three historians had described the adventure of King Charles XII when he persisted in remaining in the territories of his benefactor, the sultan, in opposition to the orders of that monarch, and absolutely fought, with the few domestics that attended his person, against an army of Janissaries and Tartars, I should have suspended my judgment about its truth; but, having spoken to many who actually witnessed the fact, and having never heard it called in question, I cannot possibly do otherwise than believe it; because, after all, although such conduct is neither wise nor common, there is nothing in it contradictory to the laws of nature, or the character of the hero.

That which is in opposition to the ordinary course of nature ought not to be believed, unless it is attested by persons evidently inspired by the divine mind, and whose inspiration, indeed, it is impossible to doubt. Hence we are justified in considering as a paradox the assertion made under the article on "Certainty," in the great *Encyclopedia,* that we are as much bound to believe in the resuscitation of a dead man, if all Paris were to affirm it, as to believe all Paris when it states that we gained the battle of Fontenoy. It is clear that the evidence of all Paris to a thing improbable can never be equal to that evidence in favor of a probable one. These are the first principles of genuine logic. Such a dictionary as the one in question should be consecrated only to truth. . . .

Liberty of the Press

What harm can the prediction of Jean Jacques do to Russia? Any? We allow him to explain it in a mystical, typical, allegorical sense, according to custom. The nations which will destroy the Russians will be the belles-lettres, mathematics, wit, and politeness which degrade man and pervert nature.

From five to six thousand pamphlets have been printed in Holland against Louis XIV, none of which contributed to make him lose the battles of Blenheim, Turin, and Ramillies.

In general, we have as natural a right to make use of our pens as our language, at our peril, risk, and fortune. I know many books which fatigue, but I know of none which have done real evil. Theologians, or pretended politicians, cry: "Religion is destroyed, the government is lost, if you print certain truths or certain paradoxes. Never attempt to think till you have demanded permission from a monk or an officer. It is against good order for a man to think for himself. Homer, Plato, Cicero, Virgil, Pliny, Horace, never published anything but with the approbation of the doctors of the Sorbonne and of the holy Inquisition.

"See into what horrible decay the liberty of the press brought

England and Holland. It is true that they possess the commerce of the whole world, and that England is victorious on sea and land; but it is merely a false greatness, a false opulence: they hasten with long strides to their ruin. An enlightened people cannot exist."

You deceive yourself very grossly when you think that you have been ruined by books. The empire of Russia is two thousand leagues in extent, and there are not six men who are aware of the points disputed by the Greek and Latin Church. If the monk Luther, John Calvin, and the vicar Zwingli had been content with writing, Rome would yet subjugate all the states that it has lost; but these people and their adherents ran from town to town, from house to house, exciting the women, and were maintained by princes. Fury, which tormented Amata, and which, according to Virgil, whipped her like a top, was not more turbulent. Know: that one enthusiastic, factious, ignorant, supple, vehement Capuchin, the emissary of some ambitious monks, preaching, confessing, communicating, and caballing, will much sooner overthrow a province than a hundred authors can enlighten it. It was not the Koran which caused Mohammed to succeed: it was Mohammed who caused the success of the Koran.

You fear books, as certain small cantons fear violins. Let us read, and let us dance—these two amusements will never do any harm to the world.

Man

Of Man in the State of Pure Nature. What would man be in the state which we call that of pure nature? An animal much below the first Iroquois whom we found in the north of America. He would be very inferior to these Iroquois, since they knew how to light fires and make arrows. He would require ages to arrive at these two arts.

Man, abandoned to pure nature, would have, for his language, only a few inarticulate sounds; the species would be reduced to a very small number, from the difficulty of getting nourishment and the want of help, at least in our harsh climates. He would have no more knowledge of God and the soul than of mathematics; these ideas would be lost in the care of procuring food. The race of beavers would be infinitely preferable. . . .

Between men of pure instinct and men of genius floats this immense number occupied solely with subsisting.

This subsistence costs us so much pains, that in the north of America an image of God often runs five or six leagues to get a dinner; whilst among us the image of God bedews the ground with the sweat of his brow, in order to procure bread.

Add to this bread—or the equivalent—a hut, and a poor dress, and you will have man such as he is in general, from one end of the universe to the other: and it is only in a multitude of ages that he has been able to arrive at this high degree of attainment.

Finally, after other ages, things got to the point at which we see them. Here we represent a tragedy in music; there we kill one another on the high seas of another hemisphere, with a thousand pieces of cannon. The opera and a ship of war of the first rank always astonish my imagination. I doubt whether they can be carried much farther in any of the globes with which the heavens are studded. More than half the habitable world, however, is still peopled with two-footed animals who live in the horrible state approaching to pure nature, existing and clothing themselves with difficulty, scarcely perceiving that they are unfortunate, and living and dying almost without knowing it. . . .

Matter

When wise men are asked what is the soul they answer that they know not. If they are asked what matter is, they make the same reply. It is true that there are professors, and particularly scholars, who know all this perfectly; and when they have repeated that matter has extent and divisibility, they think they have said all; being pressed, however, to say what this thing is which is extended, they find themselves considerably embarrassed. It is composed of parts, say they. And of what are these parts composed? Are the elements of the parts divisible? Then they are mute, or they talk a great deal; which are equally suspicious. Alas! of what avail have been all the subtleties of the mind since man first reasoned? Geometry has taught us many truths, metaphysics very few. We weigh matter, we measure it, we decompose it; and if we seek to advance one step beyond these gross operations, we find ourselves powerless, and before us an immeasurable abyss.

Miracles

A miracle, according to the true meaning of the word, is some-thing admirable; accordingly, all is miracle. The stupendous order of nature, the revolution of a hundred millions of worlds around a million of suns, the activity of light, the life of animals, all are grand and perpetual miracles.

According to common acceptation, we call a miracle the viola-tion of these divine and eternal laws. A solar eclipse at the time of the full moon, or a dead man walking two leagues and carrying his head in his arms, we denominate a miracle.

Many natural philosophers maintain that in this sense there are no miracles; and advance the following arguments:

A miracle is the violation of mathematical, divine, immutable, eternal laws. By the very exposition itself, a miracle is a contra-diction in terms: a law cannot at the same time be immutable and violated. But, they are asked, cannot a law, established by God Himself, be suspended by its author?

They have the hardihood to reply that it cannot; and that it is impossible a being infinitely wise can have made laws to violate them. He could not, they say, derange the machine but with a view of making it work better; but it is evident that God, all-wise and omnipotent, originally made this immense machine, the uni-verse, as good and perfect as He was able; if He saw that some imperfections would arise from the nature of matter, He provided for that in the beginning; and accordingly, He will never change anything in it. Moreover, God can do nothing without reason; but what reason could induce Him to disfigure for a time His own work?

It is done, they are told, in favor of mankind. They reply: We must presume, then, that it is in favor of all mankind; for it is impossible to conceive that the divine nature should occupy itself only about a few men in particular, and not for the whole human race; and even the whole human race itself is a very small con-cern: it is less than a small anthill in comparison with all the beings inhabiting immensity. But is it not the most absurd of all extravagances to imagine that the Infinite Supreme should, in favor of three or four hundred emmets on this little heap of earth, derange the operation of the vast machinery that moves the universe?

Power—Omnipotence

I presume every reader of this article to be convinced that the world is formed with intelligence, and that a slight knowledge of astronomy and anatomy is sufficient to produce admiration of that universal and supreme intelligence. . . .

Can the reader of himself ascertain that this intelligence is omnipotent, that is to say, infinitely powerful? Had he the slightest notion of infinity, to enable him to comprehend the meaning and extent of almighty power?

The celebrated philosophic historian David Hume says: "A weight of ten ounces is raised in a balance by another weight; this other weight therefore is more than ten ounces; but no one can rationally infer that it must necessarily be a hundredweight."

We may fairly and judiciously apply here the same argument. You acknowledge a Supreme Intelligence sufficiently powerful to form yourself, to preserve you for a limited time in life, to reward you and to punish you. Are you sufficiently acquainted with it to be able to demonstrate that it can do more than this? How can you prove by your reason that a being can do more than it has actually done?

The life of all animals is short. Could He make it longer? All animals are food for one another without exception; everything is born to be devoured. Could He form without destroying? You know not what His nature is. It is impossible, therefore, that you should know whether His nature may not have compelled Him to do only the very things He has done.

The globe on which we live is one vast field of destruction and carnage. Either the Supreme Being was able to make of it an eternal mode of enjoyment for all beings possessed of sensation, or He was not. If He was able and yet did not do it, you will undoubtedly tremble to pronounce or consider Him a maleficent being; but if He was unable to do so, do not tremble to regard Him as a power of very great extent indeed, but nevertheless circumscribed by His nature within certain limits.

. . .

If the Supreme Being had been infinitely powerful, no reason can be assigned why He should not have made creatures endowed with sensation infinitely happy; He has not in fact done so; therefore we ought to conclude that He could not do so.

All the different sects of philosophers have struck on the rock of physical and moral evil. The only conclusion that can be securely reached is that God, acting always for the best, has done the best that He was able to do.

This necessity cuts off all difficulties and terminates all disputes. We have not the hardihood to say: All is good. We say: There is no more evil than was absolutely inevitable.

Prayer (Public), Thanksgiving, Etc.

We know of no religion without prayers; even the Jews had them, although there was no public form of prayer among them before the time when they sang their canticles in their synagogues, which did not take place until a late period.

The people of all nations, whether actuated by desires or fears, have invoked the assistance of the Divinity. Philosophers, however, more respectful to the Supreme Being, and rising more above human weakness, have been habituated to substitute, for prayer, resignation. This, in fact, is all that appears proper and suitable between creature and Creator. But philosophy is not adapted to the great mass of mankind; it soars too high above the vulgar; it speaks a language they are unable to comprehend. To propose philosophy to them would be just as weak as to propose the study of conic sections to peasants or fishwomen.

Among the philosophers themselves, I know of no one besides Maximus Tyrius who has treated of this subject. The following is the substance of his ideas upon it: "The designs of God exist from all eternity. If the object prayed for be conformable to His immutable will, it must be perfectly useless to request of Him the very thing which He has determined to do. If He is prayed to for the reverse of what He has determined to do, He is prayed to to be weak, fickle, and inconstant; such a prayer implies that this is thought to be His character, and is nothing better than ridicule or mockery of Him. You either request of Him what is just and right, in which case He ought to do it, and it will be actually done without any solicitation, which in fact shows distrust of His rectitude; or what you request is unjust, and then you insult Him. You are either worthy or unworthy of the favor you implore; if worthy, He knows it better than you do yourself; if unworthy, you commit an additional crime in requesting that which you do not merit."

In a word, we offer up prayers to God only because we have made Him after our own image. We treat Him like a pasha, or a sultan, who is capable of being exasperated and appeased. In short, all nations pray to God: the sage is resigned, and obeys Him. Let us pray with the people, and let us be resigned to Him with the sage. . . .

Religion

Last night I was meditating; I was absorbed in the contemplation of nature, admiring the immensity, the courses, the relations, of those infinite globes which are above the admiration of the vulgar.

I admired still more the intelligence that presides over this vast machinery. I said to myself: A man must be blind not to be impressed by this spectacle; he must be stupid not to recognize its Author; he must be mad not to adore Him. What tribute of adoration ought I to render Him? Should not this tribute be the same throughout the extent of space, since the same Supreme Power reigns equally in all that extent?

. . .

I was wrapt in these reflections, when one of those genii who fill the spaces between worlds, came down to me. I recognized the same aerial creature that had formerly appeared to me, to inform me that the judgments of God are different from ours, and how much a good action is preferable to controversy.

He transported me into a desert covered all over with bones piled one upon another; and between these heaps of dead there were avenues of evergreen trees, and at the end of each avenue a tall man of august aspect gazing with compassion on these sad remains.

"Alas! my archangel," said I, "whither have you brought me?" "To desolation," answered he. "And who are those fine old patriarchs whom I see motionless and melancholy at the end of those green avenues, and who seem to weep over this immense multitude of dead?" "Poor human creature! thou shalt know," replied the genius, "but, first, thou must weep."

He began with the first heap. "These," said he, "are the twenty-three thousand Jews who dance before a calf, together with the twenty-four thousand who were slain while ravishing Midianitish women; the number of the slaughtered for similar offenses or mistakes amounts to nearly three hundred thousand.

"At the following avenues are the bones of Christians, butchered by one another on account of metaphysical disputes. They are divided into several piles of four centuries each; it was necessary to separate them, for had they been all together, they would have reached the sky."

"What!" exclaimed I, "have brethren thus treated their brethren; and have I the misfortune to be one of this brother-hood?"

"Here," said the spirit, "are the twelve millions of Americans slain in their own country for not having been baptized." "Ah! my God! why were not these frightful skeletons left to whiten in the hemisphere where the bodies were born, and where they were murdered in so many various ways? Why are all these abominable monuments of barbarity and fanaticism assembled here?" "For thy instruction. . . ."

.   .   .

Here I beheld a man of mild and simple mien, who appeared to me to be about thirty-five years old. He was looking with com-passion upon the distant heaps of whitened skeletons through which I had been led to the abode of the sages. I was astonished to find his feet swelled and bloody, his hands in the same state, his side pierced, and his ribs laid bare by flogging. "Good God!" said I, "is it possible that one of the just and wise should be in this state? I have just seen one who was treated in a very odious manner; but there is no comparison between his punishment and yours. Bad priests and bad judges poisoned him. Was it also by priests and judges that you were so cruelly assassinated?"

With great affability he answered—"Yes."

"And who were those monsters?"

"They were hypocrites."

"Ah! you have said all! by that one word I understand that they would condemn you to the worst of punishments. You then had proved to them, like Socrates, that the moon was not a goddess, and that Mercury was not a god?"

"No; those planets were quite out of the question. My country-men did not even know what a planet was; they were all arrant ignoramuses. Their superstitions were quite different from those of the Greeks."

"Then you wished to teach them a new religion?"

"Not at all; I simply said to them—'Love God with all your hearts, and your neighbor as yourselves; for that is all.' Judge whether this precept is not as old as the universe: judge whether I brought them a new worship. I constantly told them that I was come, not to abolish their law, but to fulfill it; I had observed all their rites; I was circumcised as they all were; I was baptized like the most zealous of them; like them I paid the corban; like them I kept the Passover; and ate, standing, lamb cooked with lettuce. I and my friends went to pray in their temple; my friends, too, frequented the temple after my death. In short, I fulfilled all their laws without one exception."

"What! could not these wretches even reproach you with having departed from their laws?"

"Certainly not."

"Why, then, did they put you in the state in which I now see you?"

"Must I tell you?—They were proud and selfish; they saw that I knew them; they saw that I was making them known to the citizens; they were the strongest; they took away my life; and such as they will always do the same, if they can, to whoever shall have done them too much justice."

"But did you say nothing, did you do nothing, that could serve them as a pretext?"

"The wicked find a pretext in everything."

"Did you not once tell them that you were come to bring, not peace, but the sword?"

"This was an error of some scribe. I told them that I brought, not the sword, but peace. I never wrote anything; what I said might be miscopied without any ill intent."

"You did not then contribute in anything, but your discourses, either badly rendered or badly interpreted, to those frightful masses of bones which I passed on my way to consult you?"

"I looked with horror on those who were guilty of all these murders."

"And those monuments of power and wealth—of pride and avarice—those treasures, those ornaments, those ensigns of greatness, which, when seeking wisdom, I saw accumulated on the way —do they proceed from you?"

"It is impossible; I and mine lived in poverty and lowliness; my greatness was only in virtue."

I was on the point of begging of him to have the goodness just to tell me who he was; but my guide warned me to refrain. He told me that I was not formed for comprehending these sublime mysteries. I conjured him to tell me only in what true religion consisted.

"Have I not told you already?—Love God and your neighbor as yourself."

"What! Can we love God and yet eat meat on a Friday?"

"I always ate what was given me; for I was too poor to give a dinner to anyone."

"Might we love God and be just, and still be prudent enough not to entrust all the adventures of one's life to a person one does not know?"

"Such was always my custom."

"Might not I, while doing good, be excused from making a pilgrimage to St. James of Compostella?"

"I never was in that country."

"Should I confine myself in a place of retirement with blockheads?"

"For my part, I always made little journeys from town to town."

"Must I take part with the Greek or with the Latin Church?"

"When I was in the world, I never made any difference between the Jew and the Samaritan."

"Well, if it be so, I take you for my only master."

Then he gave me a nod, which filled me with consolation. The vision disappeared, and I was left with a good conscience. . . .

Rights

Of the Ecclesiastical Ministry. Religion is instituted only to preserve order among mankind, and to render them worthy of the bounty of the Deity by virtue. Everything in a religion which does not tend to this object ought to be regarded as foreign or dangerous.

Instruction, exhortation, the fear of punishment to come, the promises of a blessed hereafter, prayer, advice, and spiritual consolation are the only means which churchmen can properly employ to render men virtuous on earth and happy to all eternity.

Every other means is repugnant to the freedom of reason, to the nature of the soul, to the unalterable rights of conscience, to the essence of religion, to that of the clerical ministry, and to the just rights of the sovereign.

Virtue infers liberty, as the transport of a burden implies active force. With constraint there is no virtue, and without virtue no religion. Make me a slave and I shall be the worse for it.

Even the sovereign has no right to employ force to lead men to religion, which essentially presumes choice and liberty. My opinions are no more dependent on authority than my sickness or my death. . . .

Sect

Every sect, of whatever opinion it may be, is a rallying point for doubt and error. Scotists, Thomists, Realists, Nominalists, Papists, Calvinists, Molinists, and Jansenists, are only warlike appellations.

There is no sect in geometry; we never say: a Euclidian, an Archimedian. When truth is evident, it is impossible to divide people into parties and factions. Nobody disputes that it is broad day at noon.

That part of astronomy which determines the course of the stars, and the return of eclipses, being now known, there is no longer any dispute among astronomers.

It is similar with a small number of truths, which are similarly established; but if you are a Mohammedan, as there are many men who are not Mohammedans, you may possibly be in error.

What would be the true religion if Christianity did not exist? That in which there would be no sects; that in which all minds necessarily agreed.

Now, in what doctrine are all minds agreed? In the adoration of one God, and in probity. All the philosophers who have professed a religion have said at all times: "There is a God, and He must be just." Behold then the universal religion, established throughout all time and among all men! The point then in which all agree is true; the systems in regard to which all differ are false. . . .

Toleration

Section I. What is toleration? It is the appurtenance of humanity. We are all full of weakness and errors; let us mutually pardon each other our follies—it is the first law of nature. . . .

It is clear that every private individual who persecutes a man, his brother, because he is not of the same opinion, is a monster. This admits of no difficulty. But the government, the magistrates, the princes!—how do they conduct themselves toward those who have a faith different from their own? If they are powerful foreigners, it is certain that a prince will form an alliance with them. The Most Christian Francis I will league himself with the Mussulmans against the Most Catholic Charles V. Francis I will give money to the Lutherans in Germany to support them in their rebellion against their emperor; but he will commence, as usual, by having the Lutherans in his own country burned. He pays them in Saxony from policy; he burns them in paris from policy. But what follows? Persecutions make proselytes. France will soon be filled with new Protestants. At first they will submit to be hanged; afterward they will hang in their turn. There will be civil wars; then St. Bartholomew will come; and this corner of the world will be worse than all that the ancients and moderns have ever said of hell. . . .

Section II. Of all religions, the Christian ought doubtless to inspire the most toleration, although hitherto the Christians have been the most intolerant of all men. Jesus, having deigned to be born in poverty and lowliness like his brethren, never condescended to practice the art of writing. The Jews had a law written with the greatest minuteness, and we have not a single line from the hand of Jesus. The apostles were divided on many points. St. Peter and St. Barnabas ate forbidden meats with the new stranger Christians, and abstained from them with the Jewish Christians. St. Paul reproached them with this conduct; and this same St. Paul, the Pharisee, the disciple of the Pharisee Gamaliel—this same St. Paul, who had persecuted the Christians with fury, and who after breaking with Gamaliel, became a

Christian himself—nevertheless, went afterward to sacrifice in the temple of Jerusalem, during his apostolic vacation. For eight days he observed publicly all the ceremonies of the Jewish law which he had renounced; he even added devotions and purifications which were superabundant; he completely Judaized. The greatest apostle of the Christians did, for eight days, the very things for which men are condemned to the stake among a large portion of Christian nations. . . .

If it were allowed to reason logically in matters of religion, it is clear that we ought all to become Jews, since Jesus Christ, our Savior, was born a Jew, lived a Jew, and died a Jew, and since he expressly said that he accomplished and fulfilled the Jewish religion. But it is still more clear that we ought mutually to tolerate one another, because we are all weak, irrational, and subject to change and error. A reed prostrated by the wind in the mire—ought it to say to a neighboring reed placed in a contrary direction: Creep after my fashion, wretch, or I will present a request for you to be seized and burned?

SHORT STUDIES ON ENGLISH TOPICS
(LETTERS ON THE ENGLISH)

English Commerce

Never has any people, since the fall of Carthage, been at the same time powerful by sea and land, till Venice set the example. The Portuguese, from their good fortune in discovering the passage by way of the Cape of Good Hope, have been for some time great lords on the coasts of the East Indies, but have never been very respectable in Europe. Even the United Provinces became warlike, contrary to their natural disposition, and in spite of themselves; and it can in no way be ascribed to their union among themselves, but to their being united with England, that they have contributed to hold the balance in Europe at the beginning of the eighteenth century.

Carthage, Venice, and Amsterdam were undoubtedly powerful; but their conduct has been exactly like that of merchants grown rich by traffic, who afterward purchase lands with the dignity of lordship annexed to them. Neither Carthage, Venice, nor Holland has, from a warlike and even conquering beginning, ended in a commercial nation. The English are the only people existing who have done this; they were a long time warriors before they learned to cast accounts. They were entirely ignorant of numbers when they won the battles of Agincourt, Crécy, and Poitiers, and were also ignorant that it was in their power to become corn factors and woolen drapers, two things that would certainly turn to much better account. This science also has rendered the nation at once populous, wealthy, and powerful. London was a poor country-town when Edward III conquered one half of France; and it is wholly owing to this that the English have become merchants; that London exceeds Paris in extent, and number of inhabitants; that they are able to equip and man two hundred sail of ships of war, and keep the kings who are their allies in pay. The Scottish are born warriors, and, from the purity of their air, inherit good sense. Whence comes it, then, that Scotland, under the name of a union, has become a province of England? It is because Scotland has scarcely any other commodity than coal, and that England has fine tin, excellent wool, and abounds in corn, manufactures, and trading companies.

When Louis XIV made Italy tremble, and his armies, already in possession of Savoy and Piedmont, were on the point of reducing Turin, Prince Eugene was obliged to march from the remotest parts of Germany to the assistance of the Duke of Savoy. He was in want of money, without which cities can neither be taken nor defended. He had recourse to the English merchants. In half an hour's time they lent him five millions, with which he effected the deliverance of Turin, beat the French, and wrote this short note to those who had lent him the money: "Gentlemen, I have received your money, and flatter myself I have employed it to your satisfaction."

Chancellor Bacon

It is not long since the ridiculous and threadbare question was agitated in a celebrated assembly, who was the greatest man, Caesar or Alexander, Tamerlane or Cromwell? Somebody said that it must undoubtedly be Sir Isaac Newton. This man was certainly in the right; for if true greatness consists in having received from heaven the advantage of a superior genius, with the talent of applying it for the interest of the possessor and of mankind, a man like Newton—and such a one is hardly to be met with in ten centuries—is surely by much the greatest; and those statesmen and conquerors which no age has ever been without are commonly but so many illustrious villains. It is the man who sways our minds by the prevalence of reason and the native force of truth, not they who reduce mankind to a state of slavery by brutish force and downright violence; the man who by the vigor of his mind is able to penetrate into the hidden secrets of nature, and whose capacious soul can contain the vast frame of the universe, not those who lay nature waste and desolate the face of the earth, that claims our reverence and admiration.

Therefore, as you are desirous to be informed of the great men that England has produced, I shall begin with the Bacons, the Lockes, and the Newtons. The generals and ministers will come after them in their turn.

I must begin with the celebrated Baron Verulam, known to the rest of Europe by the name of Bacon, who was the son of a certain keeper of the seals, and was for a considerable time chancellor under James I.

.   .   .

This great man is the father of experimental philosophy. It is true, wonderful discoveries had been made even before his time: the mariner's compass, the art of printing, that of engraving, the art of painting in oil, that of making glass, with the remarkably advantageous invention of restoring in some measure sight to the blind, that is, to old men, by means of spectacles; the secret of making gunpowder had also been discovered. They had gone in search of, discovered, and conquered a new world in another hemisphere. Who would not have thought that these sublime discoveries had been made by the greatest philosophers, and in times much more enlightened than ours? By no means; for all these astonishing revolutions happened in the ages of scholastic barbarity. Chance alone has brought forth almost all these inventions; it is even pretended that chance has had a great share in the discovery of America; at least, it has been believed that Christopher Columbus undertook this voyage on the faith of a captain of a ship who had been cast by a storm on one of the Caribbee islands. Be this as it will, men had learned to penetrate to the utmost limits of the habitable globe, and to destroy the most impregnable cities with an artificial thunder, much more terrible than the real; but they were still ignorant of the circulation of the blood, the weight and pressure of the air, the laws of motion, the doctrine of light and color, the number of the planets in our system, etc. And a man that was capable to maintain a thesis on the "Categories of Aristotle," the *universale a parte rei,* or suchlike nonsense was considered as a prodigy.

In a word, there was not a man who had any idea of experimental philosophy before Chancellor Bacon; and of an infinity of experiments which have been made since his time, there is hardly a single one which has not been pointed out in his book. He had even made a good number of them himself. He constructed several pneumatic machines, by which he discovered the elasticity of the air; he had long brooded over the discovery of its weight, and was even at times very near to catching it, when it was laid hold of by Torricelli. A short time after, experimental physics began to be cultivated in almost all parts of Europe. This was a hidden treasure, of which Bacon had some glimmerings, and which all the philosophers whom his promises had encouraged made their utmost efforts to lay open. We see in his book mention made in express terms of that new attraction of which Newton passes for the inventor. "We must inquire," said Bacon, "whether there be not a certain magnetic force, which operates reciprocally between the earth and other heavy bodies, between the moon and the ocean, between the planets, etc." In another place he says: "Either heavy bodies are impelled toward the center of the earth, or they are mutually attracted by it; in this latter case it is evident that the nearer falling bodies approach the earth, the more forcibly are they attracted by it." "We must try," continues he, "whether the same pendulum clock goes faster on the top of a mountain, or at the bottom of a mine. If the force of the weight diminishes on the mountain, and increases in the mine, it is probable the earth has a real attracting quality."

This precursor in philosophy was also an elegant writer, a historian, and a wit. His moral essays are in high estimation, though they seem rather calculated to instruct than to please; and as they are neither a satire on human nature, like the maxims of Rochefoucauld, nor a school of skepticism, like Montaigne; they are not so much read as these two ingenious books. . . .

3   *Hume*

David Hume (1711–1776), was born in Edinburgh and spent his life in literary and philosophical endeavor, with occasional forays into public life that carried him to Vienna, Turin, and Paris. Serene by temperament, he was the philosophe's *philosopher whose arguments for experimental reason lay at the heart of Enlightenment thought.*

In the selections that follow, from the Inquiry Concerning Human Understanding *(1748), Hume establishes that a miracle is without foundation in experience, and that without miracles there can be no religion, except on faith. He then attacks faith at its center. It is illegitimate, he argues, to reason from an imperfect order in the universe to a perfect creator, and then back to creation to explain away evil by reference to a future life. In this way we have gone beyond the evidence to fashion a theodicy, or a justification of the ways of God, whose behavior remains forever inscrutable to us and cannot be justified to man. Moreover, such theodicy when used in support of virtue is a less sure foundation for it than man's ordinary experience with good and evil which proves by result the superiority of virtue. Hume laid the ground-work for a utilitarian ethic.*

The selections are from the first edition of Hume's collected Philosophical Works *(1826) as edited by C. W. Hendel (N.Y., Liberal Arts Press, 1955).*

AN INQUIRY
CONCERNING HUMAN UNDERSTANDING

. . . A wise man, therefore, proportions his belief to the evidence. In such conclusions as are founded on an infallible experience, he expects the event with the last degree of assurance and

SOURCE. David Hume, *An Inquiry Concerning Human Understanding*, edited by Charles W. Hendel, copyright © 1955, by the Liberal Arts Press, Inc., reprinted by permission of the Liberal Arts Press Division of the Bobbs-Merrill Company, Inc.

regards his past experience as a full *proof* of the future existence of that event. In other cases he proceeds with more caution: he weighs the opposite experiments; he considers which side is supported by the greater number of experiments—to that side he inclines with doubt and hesitation; and when at last he fixes his judgment, the evidence exceeds not what we properly call "probability." All probability, then, supposes an opposition of experiments and observations where the one side is found to overbalance the other and to produce a degree of evidence proportioned to the superiority. A hundred instances or experiments on one side, and fifty on another, afford a doubtful expectation of any event, though a hundred uniform experiments, with only one that is contradictory, reasonably beget a pretty strong degree of assurance. In all cases we must balance the opposite experiments where they are opposite, and deduct the smaller number from the greater in order to know the exact force of the superior evidence.

.   .   .

A miracle is a violation of the laws of nature; and as a firm and unalterable experience has established these laws, the proof against a miracle, from the very nature of the fact, is as entire as any argument from experience can possibly be imagined. Why is it more than probable that all men must die, that lead cannot of itself remain suspended in the air, that fire consumes wood and is extinguished by water, unless it be that these events are found agreeable to the laws of nature, and there is required a violation of these laws, or, in other words, a miracle to prevent them? Nothing is esteemed a miracle if it ever happen in the common course of nature. It is no miracle that a man, seemingly in good health, should die on a sudden, because such a kind of death, though more unusual than any other, has yet been frequently observed to happen. But it is a miracle that a dead man should come to life, because that has never been observed in any age or country. There must, therefore, be a uniform experience against every miraculous event, otherwise the event would not merit that appellation. And as a uniform experience amounts to a proof, there is here a direct and full *proof,* from the nature of the fact, against the existence of any miracle, nor can such a proof be destroyed or the miracle rendered credible but by an opposite proof which is superior.

The plain consequence is (and it is a general maxim worthy

of our attention) that no testimony is sufficient to establish a miracle unless the testimony be of such a kind that its falsehood would be more miraculous than the fact which it endeavors to establish. . . .

Part II

In the foregoing reasoning we have supposed that the testimony upon which a miracle is founded may possibly amount to entire proof, and that the falsehood of that testimony would be a real prodigy. But it is easy to show that we have been a great deal too liberal in our concession, and that there never was a miraculous event established[1] on so full an evidence.

For, *first,* there is not to be found, in all history, any miracle attested by a sufficient number of men of such unquestioned good sense, education, and learning as to secure us against all delusion in themselves; of such undoubted integrity as to place them beyond all suspicion of any design to deceive others; of such credit and reputation in the eyes of mankind as to have a great deal to lose in case of their being detected in any falsehood, and at the same time attesting facts performed in such a public manner and in so celebrated a part of the world as to render the detection unavoidable—all which circumstances are requisite to give us a full assurance in the testimony of men.

Secondly, we may observe in human nature a principle which, if strictly examined, will be found to diminish extremely the assurance which we might, from human testimony, have in any kind of prodigy. The maxim by which we commonly conduct ourselves in our reasonings is that the objects of which we have no experience resemble those of which we have; that what we have found to be most usual is always most probable; and that where there is an opposition of arguments, we ought to give the preference to such as are founded on the greatest number of past observations. But though, in proceeding by this rule, we readily reject any fact which is unusual and incredible in an ordinary degree, yet in advancing further, the mind observes not always the same rule; but when anything is affirmed utterly absurd and miraculous, it rather the more readily admits of such a fact upon

---

[1] [Editions K and L: "in any history."]

account of that very circumstance which ought to destroy all its authority. The passion of *surprise* and *wonder,* arising from miracles, being an agreeable emotion, gives a sensible tendency toward the belief of those events from which it is derived. And this goes so far that even those who cannot enjoy this pleasure immediately, nor can believe those miraculous events of which they are informed, yet love to partake the satisfaction at second hand, or by rebound, and place a pride and delight in exciting the admiration of others.

With what greediness are the miraculous accounts of travelers received, their descriptions of sea and land monsters, their relations of wonderful adventures, strange men and uncouth manners? But if the spirit of religion join itself to the love of wonder, there is an end of common sense, and human testimony in these circumstances loses all pretensions to authority. A religionist may be an enthusiast and imagine he sees what has no reality; he may know his narrative to be false, and yet persevere in it with the best intentions in the world, for the sake of promoting so holy a cause.

.   .   .

Thirdly, it forms a strong presumption against all supernatural and miraculous relations that they are observed chiefly to abound among ignorant and barbarous nations; or if a civilized people has ever given admission to any of them, that people will be found to have received them from ignorant and barbarous ancestors, who transmitted them with that inviolable sanction and authority which always attend received opinions. When we peruse the first histories of all nations, we are apt to imagine ourselves transported into some new world where the whole frame of nature is disjointed, and every element performs its operations in a different manner from what it does at present. Battles, revolutions, pestilence, famine, and death are never the effect of those natural causes which we experience. Prodigies, omens, oracles, judgments quite obscure the few natural events that are intermingled with them. But as the former grow thinner every page, in proportion as we advance nearer the enlightened ages, we soon learn that there is nothing mysterious or supernatural in the case, but that all proceeds from the usual propensity of mankind toward the marvelous, and that, though this inclination may at intervals receive a check from sense and learning, it can never be thoroughly extirpated from human nature.

"It is strange," a judicious reader is apt to say, upon the perusal of these wonderful historians, "that such prodigious events never happen in our days!" But it is nothing strange, I hope, that men should lie in all ages. You must surely have seen instances enough of that frailty. You have yourself heard many such marvelous relations started which, being treated with scorn by all the wise and judicious, have at last been abandoned even by the vulgar. Be assured that those renowned lies which have spread and flourished to such a monstrous height arose from like beginnings, but being sown in a more proper soil shot up at last into prodigies almost equal to those which they relate.

. . .

I may add, as a *fourth* reason which diminishes the authority of prodigies, that there is no testimony for any, even those which have not been expressly detected, that is not opposed by an infinite number of witnesses, so that not only the miracle destroys the credit of testimony, but the testimony destroys itself. To make this the better understood, let us consider that in matters of religion whatever is different is contrary, and that it is impossible the religions of ancient Rome, of Turkey, of Siam, and of China should all of them be established on any solid foundation. Every miracle, therefore, pretended to have been wrought in any of these religions (and all of them abound in miracles), as its direct scope is to establish the particular system to which it is attributed, so has it the same force, though more indirectly, to overthrow every other system.

. . .

Upon the whole, then, it appears that no testimony for any kind of miracle has ever amounted to a probability, much less to a proof; and that, even supposing it amounted to a proof, it would be opposed by another proof derived from the very nature of the fact which it would endeavor to establish. It is experience only which gives authority to human testimony, and it is the same experience which assures us of the laws of nature. When, therefore, these two kinds of experience are contrary, we have nothing to do but to subtract the one from the other and embrace an opinion either on one side or the other with that assurance which arises from the remainder. But according to the principle here explained, this subtraction with regard to all popular religions amounts to an entire annihilation; and there-fore we may establish it as a maxim that no human testimony can have such force as to prove a miracle and make it a just foundation for any such system of religion.

. . .

Though the Being to whom the miracle is ascribed be in this case Almighty, it does not, upon that account, become a whit more probable, since it is impossible for us to know the attributes or actions of such a Being otherwise than from the experience which we have of his productions in the usual course of nature. This still reduces us to past observation and obliges us to com-pare the instances of the violation of truth in the testimony of men with those of the violation of the laws of nature by miracles, in order to judge which of them is most likely and probable. As the violations of truth are more common in the testimony con-cerning religious miracles than in that concerning any other matter of fact, this must diminish very much the authority of the former testimony and make us form a general resolution never to lend any attention to it, with whatever specious pretense it may be covered.

Lord Bacon seems to have embraced the same principles of reasoning.

"We ought [says he] to make a collection or particular history of all monsters and prodigious births or productions; and, in a word, of everything new, rare, and extraordinary in nature. But this must be done with the most severe scrutiny, lest we depart from truth. Above all, every relation must be considered as sus-picious which depends in any degree upon religion, as the prodigies of Livy: And no less so everything that is to be found in the writers on natural magic or alchemy, or such authors who seem all of them to have an unconquerable appetite for falsehood and fable."[2]

I am the better pleased with the method of reasoning here delivered, as I think it may serve to confound those dangerous friends or disguised enemies to the *Christian religion* who have undertaken to defend it by the principles of human reason. Our most holy religion is founded on *faith,* not on reason; and it is a

[2] *Novum Organum* lib. ii. aph. 29.

sure method of exposing it to put it to such a trial as it is by no means fitted to endure. To make this more evident, let us examine those miracles related in Scripture, and, not to lose ourselves in too wide a field, let us confine ourselves to such as we find in the Pentateuch, which we shall examine according to the principles of these pretended Christians, not as the word or testimony of God himself, but as the production of a mere human writer and historian. Here, then, we are first to consider a book presented to us by a barbarous and ignorant people, written in an age when they were still more barbarous, and, in all probability, long after the facts which it relates, corroborated by no concurring testimony, and resembling those fabulous accounts which every nation gives of its origin. Upon reading this book we find it full of prodigies and miracles. It gives an account of a state of the world and of human nature entirely different from the present: Of our fall from that state; of the age of man extended to near a thousand years; of the destruction of the world by a deluge; of the arbitrary choice of one people as the favorites of heaven, and that people the countrymen of the author; of their deliverance from bondage by prodigies the most astonishing imaginable —I desire anyone to lay his hand upon his heart and, after a serious consideration, declare whether he thinks that the falsehood of such a book, supported by such a testimony, would be more extraordinary and miraculous than all the miracles it relates; which is, however, necessary to make it be received according to the measures of probability above established.

What we have said of miracles may be applied without any variation to prophecies; and, indeed, all prophecies are real miracles and as such only can be admitted as proofs of any revelation. If it did not exceed the capacity of human nature to foretell future events, it would be absurd to employ any prophecy as an argument for a divine mission or authority from heaven. So that, upon the whole, we may conclude that the Christian religion not only was at first attended with miracles, but even at this day cannot be believed by any reasonable person without one. Mere reason is insufficient to convince us of its veracity. And whoever is moved by *faith* to assent to it is conscious of a continued miracle in his own person which subverts all the principles of his understanding and gives him a determination to believe what is most contrary to custom and experience.

. . . When we infer any particular cause from an effect, we must proportion the one to the other and can never be allowed to ascribe to the cause any qualities but what are exactly sufficient to produce the effect. A body of ten ounces raised in any scale may serve as a proof that the counterbalancing weight exceeds ten ounces, but can never afford a reason that it exceeds a hundred. If the cause assigned for any effect be not sufficient to produce it, we must either reject that cause or add to it such qualities as will give it a just proportion to the effect. But if we ascribe to it further qualities or affirm it capable of producing other effects, we can only indulge the license of conjecture and arbitrarily suppose the existence of qualities and energies without reason or authority.

The same rule holds whether the cause assigned be brute unconscious matter or a rational intelligent being. If the cause be known only by the effect, we never ought to ascribe to it any qualities beyond what are precisely requisite to produce the effect; nor can we, by any rules of just reasoning, return back from the cause and infer other effects from it, beyond those by which alone it is known to us.

. . .

You find certain phenomena in nature. You seek a cause or author. You imagine that you have found him. You afterwards become so enamored of this offspring of your brain that you imagine it impossible but he must produce something greater and more perfect than the present scene of things, which is so full of ill and disorder. You forget that this superlative intelligence and benevolence are entirely imaginary, or, at least, without any foundation in reason, and that you have no ground to ascribe to him any qualities but what you see he has actually exerted and displayed in his productions. Let your gods, therefore, O philosophers! be suited to the present appearances of nature and presume not to alter these appearances by arbitrary suppositions in order to suit them to the attributes which you so fondly ascribe to your deities.

. . .

Hence all the fruitless industry to account for the ill appearances of nature and save the honor of the gods, while we must acknowledge the reality of that evil and disorder with which the world so much abounds. The obstinate and intractable qualities of matter, we are told, or the observance of general laws, or some such reason, is the sole cause which controlled the power and benevolence of Jupiter and obliged him to create mankind and every sensible creature so imperfect and so unhappy. These attributes, then, are, it seems, beforehand taken for granted in their greatest latitude. And upon that supposition I own that such conjectures may, perhaps, be admitted as plausible solutions of the ill phenomena. But still I ask, why take these attributes for granted or why ascribe to the cause any qualities but what actually appear in the effect? Why torture your brain to justify the course of nature upon suppositions which, for aught you know, may be entirely imaginary, and of which there are to be found no traces in the course of nature?

. . .

I deny a providence, you say, and supreme governor of the world who guides the course of events, and punishes the vicious with infamy and disappointment, and rewards the virtuous with honor and success in all their undertakings. But surely I deny not the course itself of events, which lies open to everyone's inquiry and examination. I acknowledge that in the present order of things virtue is attended with more peace of mind than vice, and meets with a more favorable reception from the world. I am sensible that, according to the past experience of mankind, friendship is the chief joy of human life, and moderation the only source of tranquillity and happiness. I never balance between the virtuous and the vicious course of life, but am sensible that, to a well-disposed mind, every advantage is on the side of the former. And what can you say more, allowing all your suppositions and reasonings? You tell me, indeed, that this disposition of things proceeds from intelligence and design. But whatever it proceeds from, the disposition itself, on which depends our happiness or misery, and consequently our conduct and deportment in life, is still the same. It is still open for me, as well as you, to regulate my behavior by my experience of past events. And if you affirm that, while a divine providence is allowed, and a supreme distributive justice in the universe, I ought to expect some more particular reward of the good, and punishment of the bad, beyond the ordinary course of events, I here find the same fallacy which I have before endeavored to detect. You persist in imagining that if we grant that divine existence for which you so earnestly contend, you may safely infer consequences from it and add something to the experienced order of nature by arguing from the attributes which you ascribe to your gods. You seem not to remember that all your reasonings on this subject can only be drawn from effects to causes, and that every argument deduced from causes to effects must of necessity be a gross sophism, since it is impossible for you to know anything of the cause but what you have antecedently not inferred, but discovered to the full in the effect.

But what must a philosopher think of those vain reasoners who, instead of regarding the present scene of things as the sole object of their contemplation, so far reverse the whole course of nature as to render this life merely a passage to something further —a porch which leads to a greater and vastly different building, a prologue which serves only to introduce the piece and give it more grace and propriety? Whence, do you think, can such philosophers derive their idea of the gods? From their own conceit and imagination surely. For if they derive it from the present phenomena, it would never point to anything further, but must be exactly adjusted to them. That the divinity may *possibly* be endowed with attributes which we have never seen exerted, may be governed by principles of action which we cannot discover to be satisfied—all this will freely be allowed. But still this is mere *possibility* and hypothesis. We never can have reason to *infer* any attributes or any principles of action in him, but so far as we know them to have been exerted and satisfied.

Are there any marks of a distributive justice in the world? If you answer in the affirmative, I conclude that, since justice here exerts itself, it is satisfied. If you reply in the negative, I conclude that you have then no reason to ascribe justice, in our sense of it, to the gods. If you hold a medium between affirmation and negation, by saying that the justice of the gods at present exerts itself in part, but not in its full extent, I answer that you have no reason to give it any particular extent, but only so far as you see it, *at present,* exert itself.

Thus I bring the dispute, O Athenians! to a short issue with my antagonists. The course of nature lies open to my contemplation as well as to theirs. The experienced train of events is the great standard by which we all regulate our conduct. Nothing else can be appealed to in the field or in the senate. Nothing else ought ever to be heard of in the school or in the closet. In vain would our limited understanding break through those boundaries which are too narrow for our fond imagination. While we argue from the course of nature and infer a particular intelligent cause which first bestowed and still preserves order in the universe, we embrace a principle which is both uncertain and useless. It is uncertain because the subject lies entirely beyond the reach of human experience. It is useless because our knowledge of this cause being derived entirely from the course of nature, we can never, according to the rules of just reasoning, return back from the cause with any new inference or, making additions to the common and experienced course of nature, establish any principles of conduct and behavior.

. . .

There is still one circumstance, replied I, which you seem to have overlooked. Though I should allow your premises, I must deny your conclusion. You conclude that religious doctrines and reasonings *can* have no influence on life because they *ought* to have no influence, never considering that men reason not in the same manner you do, but draw many consequences from the belief of a divine existence and suppose that the Deity will inflict punishments on vice and bestow rewards on virtue beyond what appear in the ordinary course of nature. Whether this reasoning of theirs be just or not is no matter. Its influence on their life and conduct must still be the same. And those who attempt to disabuse them of such prejudices may, for aught I know, be good reasoners, but I cannot allow them to be good citizens and politicians, since they free men from one restraint upon their passions and make the infringement of the laws of society in one respect more easy and secure.

After all, I may perhaps agree to your general conclusion in favor of liberty, though upon different premises from those on which you endeavor to found it. I think that the state ought to tolerate every principle of philosophy, nor is there an instance that any government has suffered in its political interests by such indulgence. There is no enthusiasm among philosophers; their doctrines are not very alluring to the people, and no restraint can be put upon their reasonings but what must be of dangerous consequence to the sciences, and even to the state, by paving the

way for persecution and oppression in points where the generality
of mankind are more deeply interested and concerned.

But there occurs to me (continued I) with regard to your main
topic a difficulty which I shall just propose to you, without insisting on it, lest it lead into reasonings of too nice and delicate
a nature. In a word, I much doubt whether it be possible for a
cause to be known only by its effect (as you have all along supposed) or to be of so singular and particular a nature as to have
no parallel and no similarity with any other cause or object that
has ever fallen under our observation. It is only when two *species*
of objects are found to be constantly conjoined that we can infer
the one from the other; and were an effect presented which was
entirely singular and could not be comprehended under any
known *species*, I do not see that we could form any conjecture
or inference at all concerning its cause. If experience and observation, and analogy, be indeed the only guides which we can
reasonably follow in inferences of this nature, both the effect
and cause must bear a similarity and resemblance to other effects
and causes which we know, and which we have found in many
instances to be conjoined with each other. I leave it to your own
reflection to pursue the consequences of this principle. I shall just
observe that as the antagonists of Epicurus always suppose the
universe, an effect quite singular and unparalleled, to be the
proof of a Deity, a cause no less singular and unparalleled, your
reasonings upon that supposition seem at least to merit our
attention. There is, I own, some difficulty how we can ever
return from the cause to the effect and, reasoning from our ideas
of the former, infer any alteration on the latter or any addition
to it.

B.   MAN AND MORALS

1   *Diderot*

Perhaps the most noteworthy of the philosophes *for accomplishment and depth of intellect was Denis Diderot (1713–1784). At first a deist like Voltaire, Diderot gradually arrived at a position of pantheistic naturalism from which he viewed the world as a single substance—as sensitized matter in motion. The* Conversation between D'Alembert and Diderot *and* D'Alembert's Dream *reveal his materialism full blown.*

Diderot, joining Voltaire and Hume in their attack on metaphysics, defined reason not as a source of knowledge but as a process by which we attain it. Such positive knowledge as we have is authenticated by its utility to man. But Diderot departed from Voltaire in ethics. While Voltaire believed that virtue is natural to man and consequently useful to him, Diderot argued in the Supplement to Bougainville's Voyage *that whatever is natural to man, hence useful to him, is virtuous. He retreated from this position, however, in* Rameau's Nephew *where, carrying the principle to its logical extension, he notes the danger of defining virtue in terms of man's needs.*

SOURCE. *Diderot, Interpreter of Nature: Selected Writings*, translated by Jean Stewart and Jonathan Kemp. Copyright © 1963 by International Publishers. Reprinted with permission.

CONVERSATION BETWEEN
D'ALEMBERT AND DIDEROT

D'ALEMBERT: I confess that a Being who exists somewhere and yet corresponds to no point in space, a Being who, lacking extension, yet occupies space; who is present in his entirety in every part of that space, who is essentially different from matter and yet is one with matter, who follows its motion, and moves it, without himself being in motion, who acts on matter and yet is subject to all its vicissitudes, a Being about whom I can form no idea; a Being of so contradictory a nature, is a hypothesis difficult to accept. But other problems arise if we reject it; for if this faculty of sensation, which you propose as substitute, is a general and essential quality of matter, then stone must be sensitive.

DIDEROT: Why not?

D'ALEMBERT: It's hard to believe.

DIDEROT: Yes, for him who cuts, chisels, and crushes it, and does not hear it cry out.

D'ALEMBERT: I'd like you to tell me what difference there is, according to you, between a man and a statue, between marble and flesh.

DIDEROT: Not much. Flesh can be made from marble, and marble from flesh.

D'ALEMBERT: But one is not the other.

DIDEROT: In the same way that what you call animate force is not the same as inanimate force.

D'ALEMBERT: I don't follow you.

DIDEROT: I'll explain. The transference of a body from one place to another is not itself motion; it is the consequence of motion. Motion exists equally in the body displaced and in the body that remains stationary.

D'ALEMBERT: That's a new way of looking at things.

DIDEROT: True none the less. Take away the obstacle that prevents the displacement of a stationary body, and it will be transferred. Suddenly rarefy the air that surrounds the trunk of this huge oak, and the water contained in it, suddenly expanding, will burst it into a hundred thousand fragments. I say the same of your own body.

D'ALEMBERT: That may be so. But what relation is there between motion and the faculty of sensation? Do you, by any chance, distinguish between an active and an inactive sensitiveness, as between animate and inanimate force? An animate force which is revealed by displacement, an inanimate force which manifests itself by pressure; an active sensitiveness which would be characterized by a certain recognizable behavior in the animal and perhaps in the plant, while your inactive sensitiveness only makes itself known when it changes over to the active state?

DIDEROT: Precisely; just as you say.

D'ALEMBERT: So, then, the statue merely has inactive sensitiveness; and man, animals, perhaps even plants, are endowed with active sensitiveness.

DIDEROT: There is undoubtedly that difference between the marble block and living tissue; but you can well imagine that's not the only one.

D'ALEMBERT: Of course. Whatever likeness there may be in outward form between a man and a statue, there is no similarity in their internal organization. The chisel of the cleverest sculptor cannot make even an epidermis. But there is a very simple way of transforming an inanimate force into an animate one—the experiment is repeated a hundred times a day before our eyes— whereas I don't quite see how a body can be made to pass from the state of inactive to that of active sensitiveness.

DIDEROT: Because you don't want to see it. It is just as common a phenomenon.

D'ALEMBERT: And what is this common phenomenon, if you please?

DIDEROT: I'll tell you, since you want to be put to shame; it occurs every time you eat.

D'ALEMBERT: Every time I eat!

DIDEROT: Yes, for what do you do when you eat? You remove obstacles that prevented the food from possessing active sensitiveness. You assimilate it, you turn it into flesh, you make it animal, you give it the faculty of sensation. . . .

DIDEROT: If you're worried by the question "Which came first, the hen or the egg?" it's because you suppose that animals were originally the same as they are now. What madness! We can no more tell what they were originally than what they will become. The tiny worm, wriggling in the mud, may be in the process of developing into a large animal; the huge animal, that terrifies us by its size, is perhaps on the way to becoming a worm, is perhaps a particular and transient production of this planet. . . .

DIDEROT: Can you tell me what constitutes the existence of a perceiving being, for that being itself?

D'ALEMBERT: The consciousness of continued identity from the first moment of reflection to the present.

DIDEROT: And on what is this consciousness based?

D'ALEMBERT: On the memory of its actions.

DIDEROT: And without this memory?

D'ALEMBERT: Without this memory it would have no identity, since, realizing its existence only at the instant of receiving an impression, it would have no life story. Its life would be an interrupted series of sensations with nothing to connect them. . . .

DIDEROT: . . . Do you see this egg? With this you can overthrow all the schools of theology, all the churches of the earth. What is this egg? An unperceiving mass before the germ is introduced into it; and after the germ is introduced, what is it then? Still only an unperceiving mass, for this germ itself is only a crude, inert fluid. How will this mass develop into a different organization, to sensitiveness, to life? By means of heat. And what will produce the heat? Motion. What will be the successive effects of this motion? Instead of answering me, sit down and let's watch them from moment to moment. First there's a dot that quivers, a little thread that grows longer and takes on color; tissue is formed; a beak, tiny wings, eyes, feet, appear; a yellowish material unwinds and produces intestines; it is an animal. This animal moves, struggles, cries out; I hear its cries through the shell; it becomes covered with down; it sees. The weight of its head, shaking about, brings its beak constantly up against the inner wall of its prison; now the wall is broken; it comes out, it walks about, flies, grows angry, runs away, comes near again, complains, suffers, loves, desires, enjoys; it has the same affections as yourself, it performs the same actions. Are you going to assert with Descartes that it is a purely imitative machine? Little children will laugh at you, and philosophers will retort that if this be a machine, then you, too, are a machine. If you admit that between the animal and yourself the difference is merely one of organization, you will be showing good sense and reason, you will be honest; but from this there will be drawn the conclusion that refutes you; namely, that from inert matter, organized in a certain way, and impregnated with other inert matter, and given heat and motion, there results the faculty of sensation, life, memory, consciousness, passion, and thought. You have only two courses left to take: either to imagine within the inert mass of the egg a hidden element that awaited the egg's development before revealing its presence, or to assume that this invisible element crept in through the shell at a definite moment in the development. But what is this element? Did it occupy space or did it not? How did it come, or did it escape without moving? What was it doing there or elsewhere? Was it created at the instant it was needed? Was it already in existence? Was it waiting for a home? If it was homogeneous, it was material; if heterogeneous, one cannot account for its previous inertia nor its activity in the developed animal. Just listen to yourself, and you will be sorry for yourself; you will perceive that in order to avoid making a simple supposition that explains everything, namely, the faculty of sensation as a general property of matter or a product of its organization, you are giving up common sense and plunging headlong into an abyss of mysteries, contradictions, and absurdities. . . .

DIDEROT: Since an animal is a perceiving instrument, resembling any other in all respects, having the same structures, being strung with the same chords, stimulated in the same way by joy, pain, hunger, thirst, colic, wonder, terror, it is impossible that at the pole and at the equator it should utter different sounds. And so you will find that interjections are about the same in all languages, living and dead. The origin of conventional sounds must be ascribed to need and to proximity. The instrument endowed with the faculty of sensation, or the animal, has discovered by experience that when it uttered a certain sound a certain result followed outside it: feeling instruments like itself, or other animals, drew nearer, went away, asked or offered things, hurt or caressed it. All these consequences became connected in its memory and in that of others with the utterance of these sounds; and note that human intercourse consists only of sounds and actions.

D'ALEMBERT'S DREAM

The Speakers: D'ALEMBERT, MLLE DE L'ESPINASSE, DOCTOR BORDEU. . . .

MLLE DE L'ESPINASSE is describing to the DOCTOR, D'ALEMBERT'S strange behavior in his sleep.

MLLE DE L'ESPINASSE: . . . I'll go on. . . . He added, apostrophizing himself: "Take care, friend D'Alembert, you are assuming only contiguity where there exists continuity. . . . Yes, he's clever enough to tell me that. . . . And how is this continuity formed? That won't offer any difficulty to him. . . . As one drop of mercury coalesces with another drop of mercury, so one living and sensitive particle. . . . First there were two drops, after the contact there is only one. . . . Before assimilation there were two particles, afterward there was only one. . . . Sensitiveness becomes a common property of the common mass. . . . And, indeed, why not? I may imagine the animal fiber divided up into as many sections as I please, but that fiber will be continuous, will be a whole, yes, a whole. . . . Continuity arises from the contact of two perfectly homogeneous particles; and this constitutes the most complete union, cohesion, combination, identity, that can be imagined. . . . Yes, philosopher, if these particles are elementary and simple; but what if they are aggregates, what if they are compound? . . . They will combine none the less, and in consequence become united, continuous. . . . And then there is continual action and reaction. . . . It is certain that contact between two living particles is quite different from contiguity between two inert masses. . . . Let that pass; it might be possible to start a quarrel with you on that point; but I don't care to do so, I don't like carping. . . . Let's go back to where we were. A thread of purest gold, I remember, was one comparison he used; a homogeneous network between the particles of which others thrust themselves and form, it may be, another unified network, a tissue of sensitive matter; contact involving assimilation; sensitiveness, active in one case, inert in another, which is communicated like motion, not to mention that, as he very well put it, there must be a difference between the contact of two sensitive particles and the contact of two that are not sensitive; and wherein can that difference lie? . . . A continual action and reaction . . . and this action and reaction having a particular character. . . . Everything, then, concurs to produce a sort of unity which exists only in the animal. . . . Well! if that's not truth it's very like it. . . ." Doctor, you're laughing; can you see any sense in this?

BORDEU: A great deal. . . .

MLLE DE L'ESPINASSE: Then he began to mutter something or

other about grains, strips of flesh put to macerate in water, different and successive races of creatures that he beheld being born and passing away. With his right hand he had imitated the tube of a microscope, and with his left, I think, the mouth of a vessel. He was looking into this vessel through the tube and saying: "Voltaire can make fun of it as much as he likes, but the 'Eel Man' [Dr. Needham] is right; I believe my eyes; I can see them; what a lot they are! How they come and go, how they wriggle!" The vessel in which he perceived so many short-lived generations he compared to the universe: he saw the history of the world in a drop of water. This idea seemed a tremendous one to him; it appeared to fit in perfectly with sound philosophy, which studies great bodies in little ones. He said: "In Needham's drop of water, everything occurs and passes away in the twinkling of an eye. In the world, the same phenomenon lasts a little longer; but what is our duration compared with the eternity of time? Less than the drop I have taken up on the point of a needle compared with the limitless space that surrounds me. An unbounded series of animalcules in the fermenting atom, the same unbounded series of animalcules in this other atom that is called the earth. Who knows what races of animals have preceded us? Who knows what races of animals will come after ours? Everything changes and everything passes away, only the whole endures. The world is forever beginning and ending; each instant is its first and its last; it never has had, it never will have, other beginning or end. In this vast ocean of matter, not one molecule is like another, no molecule is for one moment like itself. *Rerum novus nascitur ordo* [a new order of things comes into being] is eternally inscribed upon it."

. . .

D'ALEMBERT: No. . . . Don't you agree that everything is connected in nature, and that it is impossible that there should be a missing link in the chain? Then what do you mean by your individuals? There aren't any, no there aren't any. . . . There is only one great individual; that is the whole. In that whole, as in a machine or some animal, you may give a certain name to a certain part, but if you call this part of the whole an individual, you are making as great a mistake as if you called the wing of a bird, or a feather on that wing, an individual. . . . And you talk of essences, poor philosophers! leave your essences out of it.

Consider the general mass, or if your imagination is too feeble to
embrace that, consider your first origin and your later end. . . .
O Architas! you who measured the globe, what are you? A handful
of ashes. . . . What is a being? The sum of a certain number of
tendencies. . . . Can I be anything other than a tendency? . . .
No, I am moving toward an end. And species? Species are only
tendencies toward a common end which is peculiar to them. . . .
And life? . . . Life, a succession of actions and reactions. . . .
Living, I act and react as a mass; . . . dead, I act and react in the
form of molecules. . . . Then I do not die? . . . No, no doubt,
I don't die in that sense, neither I myself nor anything else. . . .
Birth, life, decay, are merely changes of form. . . . And what
does the form matter? Each form has the happiness and misfortune which pertain to it. . . . From the elephant to the flea,
from the flea to the sensitive living atom, the origin of all, there
is no point in nature but suffers and enjoys. . . .

BORDEU: You see, Mademoiselle, that when we examine our sensations in general, which are all merely a differentiated sense of
touch, we must neglect the successive forms assumed by the network [nervous system] and consider only the network itself.

MLLE DE L'ESPINASSE: Every filament of the sensitive network can
be hurt or stimulated along its whole length. Pleasure or pain is
here or there, in one spot or another along the prolonged legs of
my spider, for I always come back to my spider . . . [likened to
the brain]; that spider is the common origin of all the legs and
their prolongations, and refers the pain or the pleasure to such
and such a place without feeling it.

BORDEU: It is the constant and unvarying communication of all
impressions to this common origin which constitutes the unity of
the animal.

MLLE DE L'ESPINASSE: It is the recollection of all these successive
impressions which makes up, for each animal, the story of its life
and of its individual being.

BORDEU: While memory, and the process of comparison, which
inevitably result from all these impressions, form thought and
reasoning power.

MLLE DE L'ESPINASSE: And where does this process of comparison
take place?

BORDEU: At the origin of the network.

MLLE DE L'ESPINASSE: And this network? . . .

BORDEU: Has, at its origin, no sense peculiarly its own; it does not see, hear, or suffer. It is produced and nourished; it emanates from a soft, insensitive, inert substance, that serves it as a pillow, seated on which it listens, judges, and decides.

MLLE DE L'ESPINASSE: It feels no pain?

BORDEU: No; the slightest pressure cuts short its power to judge and the whole animal falls into a deathlike condition. Remove the pressure, and the judge resumes its functions, and the animal lives again. . . .

D'ALEMBERT: [he is awake]: Doctor, one word more and then I send you to your patient. Through all the changes I have undergone in the course of my existence, perhaps not having now a single one of the molecules which formed me at birth, how have I maintained my identity for others and for myself?

BORDEU: You told us yourself in your dream.

D'ALEMBERT: Have I been dreaming?

MLLE DE L'ESPINASSE: All night long, and it sounded so like delirium that I sent for the doctor this morning.

D'ALEMBERT: And all because a certain spider's legs were mov' g of their own accord, kept the spider on the watch, and made the animal talk. And what did the animal say?

BORDEU: That it was through memory that he maintained his identity for others and for himself; and, let me add, through the slowness of the changes. If you had passed in the twinkling of an eye from youth to decay, you would have been thrown into the world as at the first moment of birth; you would not have been yourself in your own eyes, nor in those of others; while they would not have been themselves in your eyes. All connecting links would have been destroyed; all that makes up the history of your life for me, all that makes up the history of my life for you, thrown into confusion. How could you have known that this man, leaning on a stick, his eyes grown dim, dragging himself along with difficulty, and even more unlike himself inwardly than outwardly, was the same who, the day before, walked so lightly, lifted heavy burdens, gave himself up to the deepest meditations, the pleasantest and the most strenuous forms of exercise? You would not have understood your own works, you would not have recognized yourself nor anyone else, and no one would have recognized you; all the world's scene would have changed. Consider that there was less difference between yourself at birth and yourself in youth than there would be between yourself as a young man and your-self grown suddenly decrepit. Consider that, although your birth was linked to your youth by an unbroken series of sensations, yet the first three years of your life form no part of your life story. Then what would the days of your youth have meant to you if nothing linked them to the period of your decay? D'Alembert grown old would not have the slightest recollection of D'Alembert young.

MLLE DE L'ESPINASSE: In the cluster of bees, not one would have had time to take on the spirit of the whole.

D'ALEMBERT: What's that you're saying?

MLLE DE L'ESPINASSE: I am saying that the monastic spirit is preserved because the monastery repeoples itself gradually, and when a new monk enters it he finds a hundred old ones, who induce him to think and feel as they do. When one bee goes, its place in the cluster is taken by another that rapidly adapts itself.

. . .

MLLE DE L'ESPINASSE: One moment, Doctor; let us recapitulate. According to your principles, it seems to me that by a series of purely mechanical operations, I could reduce the greatest genius on earth to an unorganized mass of flesh, which would only retain the faculty of momentary sensation, and that this formless mass could then be brought back from the state of the most utter stu-pidity imaginable, to the condition of a man of genius. One of these two processes would consist in depriving the original skein of a certain number of its fibers, and thoroughly confusing the rest; and the inverse process, in restoring to the skein the fibers one had removed, and then leaving the whole to a lucky develop-ment. For instance: I take away from Newton the two auditory fibers, and he has no more sense of sound; the olfactory fibers, and he has no more sense of smell; the optic fibers, and no more sense of color; the fibers that form the palate, and he loses his sense of taste; I suppress or entangle the others, and there's an end to the organization of the brain, memory, judgment, desire, aver-sion, passion, will, self-consciousness, and behold an amorphous mass which has retained only life and sensitiveness.

BORDEU: Two qualities which are almost identical; life pertains to the aggregate, sensitiveness to the elements.

MLLE DE L'ESPINASSE: I take up this mass again and I restore to it the olfactory fibers, and it can smell; the auditory fibers, and it can hear; the optic fibers, and it can see; the fibers of the palate, and it can taste. Disentangling the rest of the skein, I allow the other fibers to develop, and I behold the rebirth of memory, of the faculty of comparison, of judgment, reason, desire, aversion, passion, natural aptitude, talent, and I find my man of genius once more, without the intervention of any heterogeneous or unintelligible agent.

BORDEU: Excellent; keep to that, all the rest is senseless verbiage. . . .

D'ALEMBERT: And abstract ideas?

BORDEU: They don't exist; there are only habitual omissions, ellipses, that make propositions more general and speech swifter and more convenient. It is the symbols of speech that have given rise to the abstract sciences. A quality common to several beings engendered the terms ugliness and beauty. We first said one man, one horse, two animals; then we said one, two, three, and the whole science of numbers was born. It is impossible to conceive of an abstract word. It was observed that all bodies have three dimensions, length, breadth, and depth; each of these was studied, and hence arose all mathematical sciences. An abstraction is merely a symbol emptied of its idea. The idea has been excluded by separating the symbol from the physical object, and it is only when the symbol is attached once more to the physical object that science becomes a science of ideas again; hence the need, so frequently felt both in conversation and in books, of having recourse to examples. When, after a long series of symbols, you ask for an example, you are only requiring the speaker to give body, shape, reality, to attach an idea to the series of sounds made by his speech, by connecting those sounds with sensations that have been experienced. . . .

SUPPLEMENT TO BOUGAINVILLE'S "VOYAGE"
OR
DIALOGUE BETWEEN A AND B

On the Disadvantage of Attaching Moral Ideas
to Certain Physical Actions Incompatible Therewith

II THE OLD MAN'S FAREWELL

He was the father of a large family. At the arrival of the
Europeans, he looked disdainfully at them, showing neither
astonishment, fear, nor curiosity. They accosted him. He turned
his back on them and withdrew into his hut. His silence and his
anxiety revealed his thoughts only too well: he lamented within
himself for the great days of his country, now eclipsed. At the
departure of Bougainville, when the inhabitants ran in a crowd
to the shore, clinging to his garments, embracing his companions
and weeping, the old man came forward with a stern air and said:

"Weep, poor folk of Tahiti, weep! Would that this were the
arrival and not the departure of these ambitious and wicked men.
One day you will know them better. One day they will return, in
one hand the piece of wood you now see attached to the belt of
this one, and the other grasping the blade you now see hanging
from the belt of another. And with these they will enslave you,
murder you or subject you to their extravagances and vices. One
day you will serve under them, as corrupted, as vile, as loathsome
as themselves. . . .

"And you, chief of these brigands who obey you, quickly take
your vessel from our shores. We are innocent, we are happy; and
you can only spoil our happiness. We follow the pure instincts of
nature; and you have tried to wipe its impress from our souls.
Here everything belongs to everybody. You have preached to us
I know not what distinctions between 'mine' and 'thine.' Our
daughters and our wives are common to us all. You have shared
this privilege with us; and you have lighted passions in them
before unknown. They have become maddened in your arms; you
have become ferocious in theirs. They have begun to hate each
other; you have slain each other for them, and they have returned
to us stained with your blood.

"We are a free people; and now you have planted in our country the title deeds of our future slavery. You are neither god nor

demon; who are you, then, to make slaves? Orou! You understand
the language of these men, tell us all, as you have told me, what
they have written on this sheet of metal—'This country is ours.'
This country yours? And why? Because you have walked thereon?
If a Tahitian landed one day on your shores, and scratched on one
of your rocks or on the bark of your trees: 'This country belongs
to the people of Tahiti'—what would you think?

"You are the strongest! And what of that? .When someone took
one of the contemptible trifles with which your vessel is filled, you
cried out and you were revenged. Yet at the same time in the
depths of your heart you plotted the theft of a whole country!
You are not a slave; you would suffer death rather than be one;
yet you want to enslave us. Do you think the Tahitian does not
know how to defend his liberty and to die? The Tahitian you
want to seize like a wild animal is your brother. You are both
children of nature; what right have you over him that he has not
over you? When you came, did we rush upon you, did we pillage
your ship? Did we seize you and expose you to the arrows of our
enemies? Did we yoke you with the animals for toil in our fields?
No. We respected our own likeness in you. Leave us to our ways;
they are wiser and more honest than yours. We do not want to
barter what you call our ignorance for your useless civilization.
Everything that is necessary and good for us we possess. Do we
deserve contempt because we have not known how to develop
superfluous wants? When we hunger we have enough to eat; when
we are cold we have wherewith to clothe us. You have been in our
huts; what is lacking there, in your opinion? You may pursue as
far as you like what you call the comforts of life; but allow sensible people to stop when they would only have obtained imaginary
good from the continuation of their painful efforts. If you
persuade us to exceed the narrow limits of our wants, when shall
we ever finish toiling? When shall we enjoy ourselves? We have
reduced the sum of our annual and daily labors to the least
possible, because nothing seems to us preferable to repose. Go to
your own country to agitate and torment yourself as much as you
like; leave us in peace. Do not worry us with your artificial needs
nor with your imaginary virtues. Look on these men; see how
upright, healthy, and robust they are. Look on these women; see
how upright, healthy, fresh, and beautiful they are. Take this
bow; it is my own. Call one, two, three, or four of your friends to

help you and try to bend it. I can bend it myself, alone. I till the soil. I climb mountains. I pierce the forest. I can run a league on the plains in less than an hour. Your young companions would be hard put to follow me, yet I am more than ninety years old.

"Woe unto this island! Woe to these people of Tahiti and to all who will come after them, woe from the day you first visited us! . . ."

IV CONTINUATION OF THE DIALOGUE

B: . . . You see, here the good almoner [chaplain] complains of the briefness of his stay in Tahiti, and of the difficulty of knowing better the customs of a people wise enough to have stopped themselves of their own accord at a median level of development, or happy enough to live in a climate where the fertility assures them a long, torpid existence, active enough to provide the necessities of life, and sufficiently indolent for their innocence, repose, and happiness to have nothing to fear from a too rapid progress of enlightenment. Nothing was evil there by law or opinion, there was only what was evil in itself. Labor and the harvests were done collectively. The accepted meaning of the word property was very narrow. The passion of love, reduced there to a simple physical appetite, produced none of our disturbances. The whole island seemed like one large family, where each hut represented the different apartments of one large mansion. He ends by declaring that these Tahitians will always be in his thoughts, that he was tempted to fling his vestments into the ship and pass the rest of his days among them, and that he feared very much that he would rue more than once not having done so.

A: But in spite of all this praise, what useful conclusions are to be drawn from the strange manners and customs of an uncivilized people?

B: I see that as soon as some physical causes, for example, the necessity for conquering the barrenness of the soil, have stimulated man's sagacity, this impetus carries him much beyond his immediate objective, and that when the period of need has passed, he is carried off into the limitless realm of fantasy, from which there is no coming back. May the happy people of Tahiti stay where they are! I see that except in this remote corner of our globe, there has never been morality and perhaps never will be anywhere.

A: Then what do you understand by morality?

B: I understand a general submission, and a conduct consequent on good or bad laws. If the laws are good, morals are good; if the laws are bad, morals are bad; if laws, good or bad, are not observed at all, that worst condition of a society, then there is no morality at all. Now, how can laws be observed if they contradict one another? Examine the history of various epochs and nations, both ancient and modern, and you will find men subjected to three codes of law, the laws of nature, civil law, and the law of religion, and constrained to infringe alternately all these codes, which have never been in agreement. From this it follows that there has never been in any country, as Orou guessed of ours, either man, or citizen, or truly pious person.

A: From which you conclude, no doubt, that in basing morality on the eternal relations which exist between men, the law of religion may become superfluous, and that civil law ought only to be the enunciation of the laws of nature.

B: And that, under pain of multiplying the wicked instead of making the good.

A: Or that if it be judged necessary to keep all three codes, the last two should only be exact copies of the first, which we carry always graven in our hearts and which will always be the most powerful.

B: That's not very exact. We have at birth only a similarity of organization with other beings, the same needs, an attraction toward the same pleasures, a common aversion for the same pains; that is what makes man as he is, and which ought to be the basis of the morality suitable for him.

A: That's not easy.

B: It is so difficult that I would willingly believe the most primitive people on earth, a Tahitian, who has held scrupulously to the laws of nature, nearer to a good code of laws than any civilized people.

A: Because it is easier for him to get rid of his too-great primitiveness than it is for us to retrace our steps and remedy our abuses.

. . .

B: We must speak against insane laws until they are reformed; while waiting, we must submit to them. Anyone who infringes a bad law by his own private authority authorizes all others to infringe the good ones. There is less inconvenience in being mad among madmen than in being wise alone. Let us tell ourselves, let us cry out unceasingly, that shame, punishment, and dishonor have been attached to actions innocent in themselves; but let us not commit these actions, because shame, punishment, and dishonor are the greatest of all evils. Let us copy the good almoner, a monk in France, a primitive man in Tahiti.

A: Take the dress of the country one's going to, and keep that of the country where one is.

B: And above all be scrupulously honest and sincere with those fragile beings who cannot delight us without renouncing the most precious advantages of our society. . . . And now, what's become of that fog?

A: It has disappeared.

RAMEAU'S NEPHEW

HE: And then, there's poverty. The voice of conscience and honor is very weak when the bowels are crying out. It's enough that if I ever grow rich, I shall certainly have to make restitution, and that I'm firmly resolved to do so in every possible way, through good fare, gaming, wine, and women.

I: But I fear you'll never grow rich.

HE: I suspect as much.

I: However, if things should turn out otherwise, what would you do?

HE: I should believe as all reclad beggars do; I should be the most insolent rascal ever seen. It's then that I should remember all they made me suffer; and I should pay them back for all the outrages they inflicted on me. I love to give orders, and I shall give them. I love to be praised, and people shall praise me. I shall have the whole of Vilmorien's gang in my service, and I shall say to them, as they said to me, "Now then, rogues, amuse me," and they will amuse me. "Get your claws into honest folks," and the honest folks, if there are any left, will be torn to shreds. And then we shall have women; we'll call each other "thou" when we are drunk; we shall get drunk; we'll tell tall stories; we'll have all sorts of perversions and vices. It will be delicious. We shall prove that Voltaire has no genius; that Buffon, always mounted on stilts, is just an inflated ranter; that Montesquieu is nothing but a society wit; we shall pack D'Alembert back to his mathematics; we shall rain blows on all you little Catos who despise us out of envy, in whom modesty is the cloak of pride, and who are sober from sheer necessity. And as for music, then's the time we shall make music!

I: From the noble use you'd make of your riches, I can see what a pity it is that you should be a beggar. Such a way of living would contribute greatly to the honor of the human race, to the benefit of your fellow citizens, and to your own glory!

HE: I believe you are laughing at me, master philosopher. You don't know with whom you are dealing; you don't suspect that I represent the most important section of society, in town and at court. All our rich folks, in every profession, may or may not have said to themselves just what I've been telling you in confidence; but the fact is that the life which I should lead, were I in their shoes, is exactly the life they do lead. I'll tell you what you're like, you fellows, you think that the same happiness suits everyone. What a strange fantasy! Your sort of happiness presupposes a certain romantic turn in mind which we haven't got, an unusual temperament, peculiar tastes. You decorate this eccentricity with the name of virtue; you call it philosophy. But do virtue and philosophy suit everyone? He has them who can, and maintains them if he can. Imagine the universe grown wise and philosophical; admit that it would be devilish dull! Look here, long live philosophy, long live the wisdom of Solomon: to drink good wine, to guzzle delicate food, tumble pretty women, and rest on soft beds! Except for this, all is vanity.

I: Ah! But to defend one's country?

HE: Vanity. There's no longer any such thing as one's country. From one pole to the other I can see only tyrants and slaves.

I: To help one's friends?

HE: Vanity. Does one have friends? And if one had them, ought one to make them guilty of ingratitude? For, look at it closely, you'll see that is all one's reward for services rendered. Gratitude is a burden; and all burdens are meant to be shaken off.

I: To have some position in society and fulfill the duties thereof?

HE: Vanity. What does it matter whether or not one has a position, so long as one is rich; since one only takes up the position in order to become rich? And where does fulfilling one's duties lead to? To jealousy, trouble, persecution. Is that how one gets on in the world? No, good heavens, but by playing the courtier, frequenting great folks, studying their tastes, humoring their whims, pandering to their vices, subscribing to their unjust actions; there's the secret. . . .

HE: . . . Everything has its right price in this world. There are two public prosecutors; one, at your door, chastises crimes against society. Nature is the other. She takes cognizance of all vices that the law lets slip. You are given to sexual excesses; very well, you shall have the dropsy. You indulge in debauchery; you shall have consumption. You open wide your doors to scoundrels, and live amongst them; you shall be betrayed, made mock of, despised. The best thing is to be resigned to the fairness of these sentences, and to say to oneself "you deserved that"; to shake one's ears and either correct one's faults or remain as one is, but on the aforesaid conditions. . . .

I: It seems to me that pleasing talents, even though second-rate, amid a people without morals and sunk in debauchery and luxury, carry a man quickly forward in the path of fortune. I myself have heard the following conversation between a sort of patron and a sort of protégé. The latter had been advised to apply to the former, as being an obliging man who might help him. "Monsieur, what do you know?"

"I know mathematics tolerably well."

"Well, then, teach mathematics; after you've covered yourself with mud on the pavements of Paris for ten or twelve years, you'll have three or four hundred livres a year."

"I've studied law, and I am well versed in jurisprudence."

"If Puffendorf and Grotius came back into the world, they would die of hunger, propped up against a milestone."

"I have a good knowledge of history and geography."

"If there were any parents who took their children's education seriously, your fortune would be made, but there aren't any."

"I'm a fairly good musician."

"Well! Why didn't you say that at first? And to show you that profit can be got from that talent, I have a daughter. Come every day, from half past seven till nine in the evening; you shall give her lessons, and I will give you twenty-five louis a year. You shall breakfast, dine, lunch, and sup with us. The rest of your day will be your own; you may dispose of it to your own advantage."

HE: And what became of this man?

I: If he had been wise, he'd have made his fortune, which apparently is the only thing you have eyes for.

HE: Undoubtedly. Gold, gold. Gold is everything, and all the rest, without gold, is nothing. And so, instead of stuffing his [a child's] head with fine maxims, which he'd have to forget on pain of being nothing but a beggar, when I possess a sovereign, which doesn't happen often, I stand in front of him. I pull the sovereign from my pocket; I show it to him with admiration. I raise my eyes to heaven. I kiss the sovereign in front of him. And to make him understand still better the importance of the sacred coin, I speak to him in a lisping voice; I point out with my finger all that one can buy with it, a pretty frock, a pretty cap, a nice cake. Then I put the sovereign in my pocket. I walk about proudly; I lift up the flap of my waistcoat; I pat my pocket with my hand; and that's how I make him understand that the self-confidence he sees in me springs from the sovereign that's in there.

I: Nothing could be better. But if it should happen that, deeply impressed with the value of the sovereign, one day. . . .

HE: I follow you. One must shut one's eyes to that possibility. There's no moral principle but has its disadvantage. At the worst, it means a bad quarter of an hour and then all's over.

I: Even from your point of view, so wise and courageous, I persist in believing that it would be a good thing to make a musician of him. I know no quicker method of getting into touch with those in power, of serving their vices and putting one's own to profit.

HE: True; but I have schemes for a swifter and surer success. Ah! If only he were a girl! But just as one doesn't do what one pleases, so one has to accept what comes; to profit by it as much as possible; and to that end one should not be so foolish as to give a spartan education to a child destined to live in Paris, like so many fathers, who could do nothing worse if they planned disaster for their children. If my child's education is bad, that is the fault of my country's morals, and not mine. Let who can be responsible. I want my son to be happy; or, what comes to the same thing, to be honored, rich, and powerful. I have some knowledge of the easiest ways to attain this end; and I'll teach him these early. If you blame me, all you wise men, the crowd and my success will absolve me. He will have gold, you may take my word for it. If he has enough of it, he'll lack nothing, not even your esteem and your respect.

ı: Maybe you're wrong.

HE: Or else he'll do without them, like many others.

In all this, there were a great many of those things that people think, and according to which they act, but which they never say. To tell the truth, that was the most marked difference between this fellow and most of those around us. He admitted the vices that he had, and that others have; but he was no hypocrite. He was neither less nor more abominable than they; he was only franker and more consistent, and sometimes profound in his depravity. I shuddered to think what his child would become under such a teacher. It is certain that, brought up according to ideas so strictly modeled on our morality, he was bound to go far, unless something checked his progress prematurely.

2   *Kant*

Immanuel Kant (1724–1804), lived most of his life in Konigsberg where he was born, and where he lectured often at the university. His work unites the Cartesian and Humean elements in eighteenth-century thought, and is at once the capstone of the Enlightenment and the forerunner of nineteenth-century philosophy.

In the Fundamental Principles of the Metaphysics of Morals *(1785), Kant demonstrates the practicality of a rational foundation for morality; for only through reason can morality be binding on men everywhere. Here he sounds the keynote of the Enlightenment: the preeminence of reason in respect to the primacy of ethics. Kant was well aware, however, of the existence of the passions that exercise a more considerable influence over man than his reason does. He argues accordingly that man is both subject and object in the world, subject inasmuch as he chooses to obey universal laws of his own rational devising, and object as he simply obeys the laws of nature. Consequently, if*

SOURCE. Immanuel Kant, *Fundamental Principles of the Metaphysics of Morals,* translated by Thomas K. Abbott, copyright 1949, The Liberal Arts Press, Inc. Reprinted by permission of the Liberal Arts Press Division of the Bobbs-Merrill Company, Inc.

*we mean to be moral, it must be reason that prescribes our obliga-
tions to humanity, and by that token contributes to our freedom
from mere appetite. This view of morality was common to
utilitarian philosophy as well, although reason functions there in
a different role. Kantian or utilitarian, the ethics of the Enlightenment were humanist in point of origin, experimental in character,
and tended to magnify man's dignity while extending his freedom, rather than reduce him to the level of his material existence,
as so much of contemporary ethics does.*

*The work excerpted here has been translated by Thomas K.
Abbot, and reprinted by the Library of Liberal Arts.*

PREFACE

. . . As my concern here is with moral philosophy, I limit the
question suggested to this: whether it is not of the utmost necessity to construct a pure moral philosophy, perfectly cleared of
everything which is only empirical, and which belongs to anthropology? For that such a philosophy must be possible is evident
from the common idea of duty and of the moral laws. Everyone
must admit that if a law is to have moral force, that is, to be the
basis of an obligation, it must carry with it absolute necessity;
that, for example, the precept, "Thou shalt not lie," is not valid
for men alone, as if other rational beings had no need to observe
it; and so with all the other moral laws properly so called; that,
therefore, the basis of obligation must not be sought in the nature
of man, or in the circumstances in the world in which he is placed,
but *a priori* simply in the conceptions of pure reason; and
although any other precept which is founded on principles of
mere experience may be in certain respects universal, yet in as
far as it rests even in the least degree on an empirical basis, perhaps only as to a motive, such a precept, while it may be a
practical rule, can never be called a moral law.

Thus not only are moral laws with their principles essentially
distinguished from every other kind of practical knowledge in
which there is anything empirical, but all moral philosophy rests
wholly on its pure part. When applied to man, it does not borrow
the least thing from the knowledge of man himself (anthropol-

ogy), but gives laws *a priori* to him as a rational being. No doubt
these laws require a judgment sharpened by experience, in order,
on the one hand, to distinguish in what cases they are applicable,
and, on the other, to procure for them access to the will of the
man, and effectual influence on conduct; since man is acted on
by so many inclinations that, though capable of the idea of a
practical pure reason, he is not so easily able to make it effective
in concreto in his life.

A metaphysic of morals is therefore indispensably necessary, not
merely for speculative reasons, in order to investigate the sources
of the practical principles which are to be found *a priori* in our
reason, but also because morals themselves are liable to all sorts
of corruption as long as we are without that clue and supreme
canon by which to estimate them correctly. For in order that
an action should be morally good, it is not enough that it *conform*
to the moral law, but it must also be done *for the sake of the law,*
otherwise that conformity is only very contingent and uncertain;
since a principle which is not moral, although it may now and
then produce actions conformable to the law, will also often produce actions which contradict it. Now it is only in a pure
philosophy that we can look for the moral law in its purity and
genuineness (and, in a practical matter, this is of the utmost
consequence): we must, therefore, begin with pure philosophy
(metaphysic), and without it there cannot be any moral philosophy at all. That which mingles these pure principles with the
empirical does not deserve the name of philosophy (for what
distinguishes philosophy from common rational knowledge is
that it treats in separate sciences what the latter only comprehends
confusedly); much less does it deserve that of moral philosophy,
since by this confusion it even spoils the purity of morals themselves and counteracts its own end.

.   .   .

FIRST SECTION:

Transition from the Common Rational
Knowledge of Morality to the Philosophical

Nothing can possibly be conceived in the world, or even out of
it, which can be called good without qualification, except a *good*

will. Intelligence, wit, judgment, and the other *talents* of the mind, however they may be named, or courage, resolution, perseverance, as qualities of temperament, are undoubtedly good and desirable in many respects; but these gifts of nature may also become extremely bad and mischievous if the will which is to make use of them, and which, therefore, constitutes what is called *character,* is not good. It is the same with the *gifts of fortune.* Power, riches, honor, even health, and the general well-being and contentment with one's condition which is called *happiness,* inspire pride, and often presumption, if there is not a good will to correct the influence of these on the mind, and with this also to rectify the whole principle of acting, and adapt it to its end. The sight of a being who is not adorned with a single feature of a pure and good will, enjoying unbroken prosperity, can never give pleasure to an impartial rational spectator. Thus a good will appears to constitute the indispensable condition even of being worthy of happiness.

. . .

There is, however, something so strange in this idea of the absolute value of the mere will, in which no account is taken of its utility, that notwithstanding the thorough assent of even common reason to the idea, yet a suspicion must arise that it may perhaps really be the product of mere high-flown fancy, and that we may have misunderstood the purpose of nature in assigning reason as the governor of our will. Therefore we will examine this idea from this point of view.

In the physical constitution of an organized being, that is, a being adapted suitably to the purposes of life, we assume it as a fundamental principle that no organ for any purpose will be found but what is also the fittest and best adapted for that purpose. Now in a being which has reason and a will, if the proper object of nature were its *conservation,* its *welfare,* in a word, its *happiness,* then nature would have hit upon a very bad arrangement in selecting the reason of the creature to carry out this purpose. For all the actions which the creature has to perform with a view to this purpose, and the whole rule of its conduct, would be far more surely prescribed to it by instinct, and that end would have been attained thereby much more certainly than it ever can be by reason. Should reason have been communicated to this favored creature over and above, it must only have served it to contemplate the happy constitution of its nature, to admire it, to congratulate itself thereon, and to feel thankful for it to the beneficent cause, but not that it should subject its desires to that weak and delusive guidance, and meddle bunglingly with the purpose of nature. In a word, nature would have taken care that reason should not break forth into *practical exercise,* nor have the presumption, with its weak insight, to think out for itself the plan of happiness and of the means of attaining it. Nature would not only have taken on herself the choice of the ends but also of the means, and with wise foresight would have entrusted both to instinct.

.   .   .

For as reason is not competent to guide the will with certainty in regard to its objects and the satisfaction of all our wants (which it to some extent even multiplies), this being an end to which an implanted instinct would have led with much greater certainty; and since, nevertheless, reason is imparted to us as a practical faculty, that is, as one which is to have influence on the *will,* therefore, admitting that nature generally in the distribution of her capacities has adapted the means to the end, its true destination must be to produce a *will,* not merely good as a *means* to something else, but *good in itself,* for which reason was absolutely necessary. This will then, though not indeed the sole and complete good, must be the supreme good and the condition of every other, even of the desire of happiness. Under these circumstances, there is nothing inconsistent with the wisdom of nature in the fact that the cultivation of the reason, which is requisite for the first and unconditional purpose, does in many ways interfere, at least in this life, with the attainment of the second, which is always conditional—namely, happiness. Nay, it may even reduce it to nothing, without nature thereby failing of her purpose. For reason recognizes the establishment of a good will as its highest practical destination, and in attaining this purpose is capable only of a satisfaction of its own proper kind, namely, that from the attainment of an end, which end again is determined by reason only, notwithstanding that this may involve many a disappointment to the ends of inclination.

We have then to develop the notion of a will which deserves to be highly esteemed for itself, and is good without a view to anything further, a notion which exists already in the sound natural understanding, requiring rather to be cleared up than to be taught, and which in estimating the value of our actions always takes the first place and constitutes the condition of all the rest. In order to do this, we will take the notion of duty, which includes that of a good will, although implying certain subjective restrictions and hindrances. These, however, far from concealing it or rendering it unrecognizable, rather bring it out by contrast and make it shine forth so much the brighter.

I omit here all actions which are already recognized as inconsistent with duty, although they may be useful for this or that purpose, for with these the question whether they are done *from duty* cannot arise at all, since they even conflict with it. I also set aside those actions which really conform to duty, but to which men have *no* direct *inclination,* performing them because they are impelled thereto by some other inclination. For in this case we can readily distinguish whether the action which agrees with duty is done *from duty* or from a selfish view. It is much harder to make this distinction when the action accords with duty, and the subject has besides a *direct* inclination to it. For example, it is always a matter of duty that a dealer should not overcharge an inexperienced purchaser; and wherever there is much commerce the prudent tradesman does not overcharge, but keeps a fixed price for everyone, so that a child buys of him as well as any other. Men are thus *honestly* served; but this is not enough to make us believe that the tradesman has so acted from duty and from principles of honesty; his own advantage required it; it is out of the question in this case to suppose that he might besides have a direct inclination in favor of the buyers, so that, as it were, from love he should give no advantage to one over another. Accordingly the action was done neither from duty nor from direct inclination, but merely with a selfish view.

On the other hand, it is a duty to maintain one's life; and, in addition, everyone has also a direct inclination to do so. But on this account the often anxious care which most men take for it has no intrinsic worth, and their maxim has no moral import. They preserve their life *as duty requires,* no doubt, but not *because duty requires.* On the other hand, if adversity and hopeless sorrow have completely taken away the relish for life, if the unfortunate one, strong in mind, indignant at his fate rather than desponding or dejected, wishes for death, and yet preserves his life without loving it—not from inclination or fear, but from duty—then his maxim has a moral worth.

. . .

The second[1] proposition is: That an action done from duty derives its moral worth, *not from the purpose* which is to be attained by it, but from the maxim by which it is determined, and therefore does not depend on the realization of the object of the action, but merely on the *principle of volition* by which the action has taken place, without regard to any object of desire. It is clear from what precedes that the purposes which we may have in view in our actions, or their effects regarded as ends and springs of the will, cannot give to actions any unconditional or moral worth. In what, then, can their worth lie if it is not to consist in the will and in reference to its expected effect? It cannot lie anywhere but in the *principle of the will* without regard to the ends which can be attained by the action. For the will stands between its *a priori* principle, which is formal, and its *a posteriori* spring, which is material, as between two roads, and as it must be determined by something, it follows that it must be determined by the formal principle of volition when an action is done from duty, in which case every material principle has been withdrawn from it.

The third proposition, which is a consequence of the two preceding, I would express thus: *Duty is the necessity of acting from respect for the law.*

. . .

The pre-eminent good which we call moral can therefore consist in nothing else than *the conception of law* in itself, *which certainly is only possible in a rational being*, in so far as this conception, and not the expected effect, determines the will. This is a good which is already present in the person who acts accordingly, and we have not to wait for it to appear first in the result.

But what sort of law can that be the conception of which must determine the will, even without paying any regard to the effect expected from it, in order that this will may be called good absolutely and without qualification? As I have deprived the will of every impulse which could arise to it from obedience to any law, there remains nothing but the universal conformity of its

---

[1] [The first proposition was that to have moral worth an action must be done from duty.]

actions to law in general, which alone is to serve the will as a principle, that is, I am never to act otherwise than so *that I could also will that my maxim should become a universal law.*

. . .

Without being an enemy of virtue, a cool observer, one that does not mistake the wish for good, however lively, for its reality, may sometimes doubt whether true virtue is actually found any-where in the world, and this especially as years increase and the judgment is partly made wiser by experience, and partly also more acute in observation. This being so, nothing can secure us from falling away altogether from our ideas of duty, or maintain in the soul a well-grounded respect for its law, but the clear conviction that although there should never have been actions which really sprang from such pure sources, yet whether this or that takes place is not at all the question; but that reason of itself, independent on all experience, ordains what ought to take place, that accordingly actions of which perhaps the world has hitherto never given an example, the feasibility even of which might be very much doubted by one who founds everything on experience, are nevertheless inflexibly commanded by reason; that, for ex-ample, even though there might never yet have been a sincere friend, yet not a whit the less is pure sincerity in friendship re-quired of every man, because, prior to all experience, this duty is involved as duty in the idea of a reason determining the will by *a priori* principles.

When we add further that, unless we deny that the notion of morality has any truth or reference to any possible object, we must admit that its law must be valid, not merely for men, but for all *rational creatures generally,* not merely under certain contingent conditions or with exceptions, but *with absolute necessity,* then it is clear that no experience could enable us to infer even the possibility of such apodictic laws.

. . .

Everything in nature works according to laws. Rational beings alone have the faculty of acting according *to the conception* of laws—that is, according to principles, that is, have a *will.* Since the deduction of actions from principles requires *reason,* the will is nothing but practical reason. If reason infallibly determines the will, then the actions of such a being which are recognized as objectively necessary are subjectively necessary also, that is, the will is a faculty to choose *that only* which reason independent on inclination recognizes as practically necessary, that is, as good. But if reason of itself does not sufficiently determine the will, if the latter is subject also to subjective conditions (particular impulses) which do not always coincide with the objective conditions, in a word, if the will does not *in itself* completely accord with reason (which is actually the case with men), then the actions which objectively are recognized as necessary are subjectively contingent, and the determination of such a will according to objective laws is *obligation,* that is to say, the relation of the objective laws to a will that is not thoroughly good is conceived as the determination of the will of a rational being by principles of reason, but which the will from its nature does not of necessity follow.

The conception of an objective principle, in so far as it is obligatory for a will, is called a command (of reason), and the formula of the command is called an Imperative.

. . .

There is therefore but one categorical imperative, namely, this: *Act only on that maxim whereby thou canst at the same time will that it should become a universal law.*

. . .

1. A man reduced to despair by a series of misfortunes feels wearied of life, but is still so far in possession of his reason that he can ask himself whether it would not be contrary to his duty to himself to take his own life. Now he inquires whether the maxim of his action could become a universal law of nature. His maxim is: From self-love I adopt it as a principle to shorten my life when its longer duration is likely to bring more evil than satisfaction. It is asked then simply whether this principle founded on self-love can become a universal law of nature. Now we see at once that a system of nature of which it should be a law to destroy life by means of the very feeling whose special nature it is to impel to the improvement of life would contradict itself, and therefore could not exist as a system of nature; hence that maxim cannot possibly exist as a universal law of nature, and consequently would be wholly inconsistent with the supreme principle of all duty.

2. Another finds himself forced by necessity to borrow money. He knows that he will not be able to repay it, but sees also that nothing will be lent to him unless he promises stoutly to repay

it in a definite time. He desires to make this promise, but he has still so much conscience as to ask himself: Is it not unlawful and inconsistent with duty to get out of a difficulty in this way? Suppose, however, that he resolves to do so, then the maxim of his action would be expressed thus: When I think myself in want of money, I will borrow money and promise to repay it, although I know that I never can do so. Now this principle of self-love or of one's own advantage may perhaps be consistent with my whole future welfare; but the question now is, Is it right? I change then the suggestion of self-love into a universal law, and state the question thus: How would it be if my maxim were a universal law? Then I see at once that it could never hold as a universal law of nature, but would necessarily contradict itself. For supposing it to be a universal law that everyone when he thinks himself in a difficulty should be able to promise whatever he pleases, with the purpose of not keeping his promise, the promise itself would become impossible, as well as the end that one might have in view in it, since no one would consider that anything was promised to him, but would ridicule all such statements as vain pretenses.

3. A third finds in himself a talent which with the help of some culture might make him a useful man in many respects. But he finds himself in comfortable circumstances and prefers to indulge in pleasure rather than to take pains in enlarging and improving his happy natural capacities. He asks, however, whether his maxim of neglect of his natural gifts, besides agreeing with his inclination to indulgence, agrees also with what is called duty. He sees then that a system of nature could indeed subsist with such a universal law, although men (like the South Sea islanders) should let their talents rest and resolve to devote their lives merely to idleness, amusement, and propagation of their species—in a word, to enjoyment; but he cannot possibly *will* that this should be a universal law of nature, or be implanted in us as such by a natural instinct. For, as a rational being, he necessarily wills that his faculties be developed, since they serve him, and have been given him, for all sorts of possible purposes.

4. A fourth, who is in prosperity, while he sees that others have to contend with great wretchedness and that he could help them, thinks: What concern is it of mine? Let everyone be as happy as Heaven pleases, or as he can make himself; I will take

nothing from him nor even envy him, only I do not wish to contribute anything to his welfare or to his assistance in distress! Now no doubt, if such a mode of thinking were a universal law, the human race might very well subsist, and doubtless even better than in a state in which everyone talks of sympathy and good-will, or even takes care occasionally to put it into practice, but, on the other side, also cheats when he can, betrays the rights of men, or otherwise violates them. But although it is possible that a universal law of nature might exist in accordance with that maxim, it is impossible to *will* that such a principle should have the universal validity of a law of nature. For a will which resolved this would contradict itself, inasmuch as many cases might occur in which one would have need of the love and sympathy of others, and in which, by such a law of nature, sprung from his own will, he would deprive himself of all hope of the aid he desires.

These are a few of the many actual duties, or at least what we regard as such, which obviously fall into two classes on the one principle that we have laid down. We must be *able to will* that a maxim of our action should be a universal law. This is the canon of the moral appreciation of the action generally. Some actions are of such a character that their maxim cannot without contradiction be even *conceived* as a universal law of nature, far from it being possible that we should *will* that it *should* be so. In others, this intrinsic impossibility is not found, but still it is impossible to *will* that their maxim should be raised to the universality of a law of nature, since such a will would contradict itself. It is easily seen that the former violate strict or rigorous (inflexible) duty; the latter only laxer (meritorious) duty. Thus it has been completely shown by these examples how all duties depend as regards the nature of the obligation (not the object of the action) on the same principle.

. . .

If then there is a supreme practical principle or, in respect of the human will, a categorical imperative, it must be one which, being drawn from the conception of that which is necessarily an end for everyone because it is *an end in itself,* constitutes an *objective* principle of will, and can therefore serve as a universal practical law. The foundation of this principle is: *rational nature exists as an end in itself.* Man necessarily conceives his own existence as being so; so far then this is a *subjective* principle of human actions. But every other rational being regards its existence similarly, just on the same rational principle that holds for me; so that it is at the same time an objective principle from which as a supreme practical law all laws of the will must be capable of being deduced. Accordingly the practical imperative will be as follows: *So act as to treat humanity, whether in thine own person or in that of any other, in every case as an end withal, never as means only.*

. . .

This principle that humanity and generally every rational nature is *an end in itself* (which is the supreme limiting condition of every man's freedom of action), is not borrowed from experience, *first,* because it is universal, applying as it does to all rational beings whatever, and experience is not capable of determining anything about them; *secondly,* because it does not present humanity as an end to men (subjectively), that is, as an object which men do of themselves actually adopt as an end; but as an objective end which must as a law constitute the supreme limiting condition of all our subjective ends, let them be what we will; it must therefore spring from pure reason. In fact the objective principle of all practical legislation lies (according to the first principle) in *the rule* and its form of universality which makes it capable of being a law (say, for example, a law of nature); but the *subjective* principle is in the *end;* now by the second principle, the subject of all ends is each rational being inasmuch as it is an end in itself. Hence follows the third practical principle of the will, which is the ultimate condition of its harmony with the universal practical reason, viz., the idea of *the will of every rational being as a universally legislative will.*

On this principle all maxims are rejected which are inconsistent with the will being itself universal legislator. Thus the will is not subject to the law, but so subject that it must be regarded *as itself giving the law,* and on this ground only subject to the law (of which it can regard itself as the author).

. . .

In the kingdom of ends everything has either *value* or *dignity.* Whatever has a value can be replaced by something else which is *equivalent;* whatever, on the other hand, is above all value, and therefore admits of no equivalent, has a dignity.

. . .

Thus morality, and humanity as capable of it, is that which alone has dignity. Skill and diligence in labor have a market value; wit, lively imagination, and humor have fancy value; on the other hand, fidelity to promises, benevolence from principle (not from instinct), have an intrinsic worth. Neither nature nor art contains anything which in default of these it could put in their place, for their worth consists not in the effects which spring from them, not in the use and advantage which they secure, but in the disposition of mind, that is, the maxims of the will which are ready to manifest themselves in such actions, even though they should not have the desired effect. These actions also need no recommendation from any subjective taste or sentiment, that they may be looked on with immediate favor and satisfaction; they need no immediate propension or feeling for them; they exhibit the will that performs them as an object of an immediate respect, and nothing but reason is required to *impose* them on the will; not to *flatter* it into them, which, in the case of duties, would be a contradiction. This estimation therefore shows that the worth of such a disposition is dignity, and places it infinitely above all value, with which it cannot for a moment be brought into comparison or competition without as it were violating its sanctity.

What then is it which justifies virtue or the morally good disposition, in making such lofty claims? It is nothing less than the privilege it secures to the rational being of participating in the giving of universal laws, by which it qualifies him to be a member of a possible kingdom of ends, a privilege to which he was already destined by his own nature as being an end in himself, and on that account legislating in the kingdom of ends; free as regards all laws of physical nature, and obeying those only which he himself gives, and by which his maxims can belong to a system of universal law to which at the same time he submits himself. . . . *Autonomy* then is the basis of the dignity of human and of every rational nature.

The three modes of presenting the principle of morality that have been adduced are at bottom only so many formulae of the very same law, and each of itself involves the other two. There is, however, a difference in them, but it is rather subjectively than objectively practical, intended, namely, to bring an idea of the reason nearer to intuition (by means of a certain analogy), and thereby nearer to feeling. All maxims, in fact, have—

1. A *form,* consisting in universality; and in this view the formula of the moral imperative is expressed thus, that the maxims must be so chosen as if they were to serve as universal laws of nature.

2. A *matter,* namely, an end, and here the formula says that the rational being, as it is an end by its own nature and therefore an end in itself, must in every maxim serve as the condition limiting all merely relative and arbitrary ends.

3. A *complete characterization* of all maxims by means of that formula, namely, that all maxims ought, by their own legislation, to harmonize with a possible kingdom of ends as with a kingdom of nature. There is a progress here in the order of the categories of *unity* of the form of the will (its universality), *plurality* of the matter (the objects, that is, the ends), and *totality* of the system of these. In forming our moral *judgment* of actions it is better to proceed always on the strict method, and start from the general formula of the categorical imperative: *Act according to a maxim which can at the same time make itself a universal law.*

.　.　.

It must be freely admitted that there is a sort of circle here from which it seems impossible to escape. In the order of efficient causes we assume ourselves free, in order that in the order of ends we may conceive ourselves as subject to moral laws; and we afterwards conceive ourselves as subject to these laws because we have attributed to ourselves freedom of will; for freedom and self-legislation of will are both autonomy, and therefore are reciprocal conceptions, and for this very reason one must not be used to explain the other or give the reason of it, but at most only for logical purposes to reduce apparently different notions of the same object to one single concept (as we reduce different fractions of the same value to the lowest terms).

One resource remains to us, namely, to inquire whether we do not occupy different points of view when by means of freedom we think ourselves as causes efficient *a priori*, and when we form our conception of ourselves from our actions as effects which we see before our eyes.

.　.　.

As a reasonable being, and consequently belonging to the intelligible world, man can never conceive the causality of his own will otherwise than on condition of the idea of freedom, for independence on the determining causes of the sensible world (an independence which reason must always ascribe to itself) is freedom. Now the idea of freedom is inseparably connected with the conception of *autonomy,* and this again with the universal principle of morality which is ideally the foundation of all actions of *rational* beings, just as the law of nature is of all phenomena.

Now the suspicion is removed which we raised above, that there was a latent circle involved in our reasoning from freedom to autonomy, and from this to the moral law, viz., that we laid down the idea of freedom because of the moral law only that we might afterwards in turn infer the latter from freedom, and that consequently we could assign no reason at all for this law, but could only [present] it as a *petitio principii* which well-disposed minds would gladly concede to us, but which we could never put forward as a provable proposition. For now we see that when we conceive ourselves as free we transfer ourselves into the world of understanding as members of it, and recognize the autonomy of the will with its consequence, morality; whereas, if we conceive ourselves as under obligation, we consider ourselves as belonging to the world of sense, and at the same time to the world of understanding.

. . .

There is no one, not even the most consummate villain, provided only that he is otherwise accustomed to the use of reason, who, when we set before him examples of honesty of purpose, of steadfastness in following good maxims, of sympathy and general benevolence (even combined with great sacrifices of advantages and comfort), does not wish that he might also possess these qualities. Only on account of his inclinations and impulses he cannot attain this in himself, but at the same time he wishes to be free from such inclinations which are burdensome to himself. He proves by this that he transfers himself in thought with a will free from the impulses of the sensibility into an order of things wholly different from that of his desires in the field of the sensibility; since he cannot expect to obtain by that wish any gratification of his desires, nor any position which would satisfy any of his actual or supposable inclinations (for this would destroy the preeminence of the very idea which wrests that wish from him), he can only expect a greater intrinsic worth of his own person. This better person, however, he imagines himself to be

when he transfers himself to the point of view of a member of the
world of the understanding, to which he is involuntarily forced
by the idea of freedom, that is, of independence on *determining*
causes of the world of sense; and from this point of view he is
conscious of a good will, which by his own confession constitutes
the law for the bad will that he possesses as a member of the
world of sense—a law whose authority he recognizes while trans-
gressing it. What he morally "ought" is then what he necessarily
"would" as a member of the world of the understanding, and is
conceived by him as an "ought" only inasmuch as he likewise
considers himself as a member of the world of sense.

. . .

But freedom is a mere *idea* [ideal conception], the objective
reality of which can in no wise be shown according to laws of
nature, and consequently not in any possible experience; and for
this reason it can never be comprehended or understood because
we cannot support it by any sort of example or analogy. It holds
good only as a necessary hypothesis of reason in a being that
believes itself conscious of a will, that is, of a faculty distinct from
mere desire (namely, a faculty of determining itself to action as
an intelligence, in other words, by laws of reason independently
on natural instincts).

. . .

The question, then, How a categorical imperative is possible,
can be answered to this extent that we can assign the only
hypothesis on which it is possible, namely, the idea of freedom;
and we can also discern the necessity of this hypothesis, and this
is sufficient for the *practical exercise* of reason, that is, for the
conviction of the *validity of this imperative,* and hence of the
moral law; but how this hypothesis itself is possible can never be
discerned by any human reason. On the hypothesis, however, that
the will of an intelligence is free, its *autonomy,* as the essential
formal condition of its determination, is a necessary consequence.

. . .

Concluding Remark

The speculative employment of reason *with respect to nature*
leads to the absolute necessity of some supreme cause of *the
world;* the practical employment of reason *with a view to freedom*

leads also to absolute necessity, but only *of the laws of the actions* of a rational being as such. Now it is an essential *principle* of reason, however employed, to push its knowledge to a consciousness of its *necessity* (without which it would not be rational knowledge). It is, however, an equally essential *restriction* of the same reason that it can neither discern the *necessity* of what is or what happens, nor of what ought to happen, unless a condition is supposed on which it is or happens or ought to happen. In this way, however, by the constant inquiry for the condition, the satisfaction of reason is only further and further postponed. Hence it unceasingly seeks the unconditionally necessary, and finds itself forced to assume it, although without any means of making it comprehensible to itself, happy enough if only it can discover a conception which agrees with this assumption. It is therefore no fault in our deduction of the supreme principle of morality, but an objection that should be made to human reason in general, that it cannot enable us to conceive the absolute necessity of an unconditional practical law (such as the categorical imperative must be). It cannot be blamed for refusing to explain this necessity by a condition, that is to say, by means of some interest assumed as a basis, since the law would then cease to be a moral law, that is, a supreme law of freedom. And thus while we do not comprehend the practical unconditional necessity of the moral imperative, we yet comprehend its *incomprehensibility,* and this is all that can be fairly demanded of a philosophy which strives to carry its principles up to the very limit of human reason.

C. POLITICS AND PROGRESS

1   *Rousseau*

Jean Jacques Rousseau (1712–1778), born in Geneva, lived among the philosophes *but was never one of them. Self-taught, sensitive, and solitary, the moral problems which privately concerned him provide the clue to his work. The* Profession of Faith of a Savoyard Vicar *(1762) tells about good and the individual.* The Social Contract *(1762) explains society and evil. In curing man of evil, however, Rousseau never intended to send him back to the state of nature as some of his critics argued, but to make him natural within society. Indeed, only in society does man have knowledge of good and evil; in the state of nature he is simply innocent.*

The Savoyard Vicar discovers through his feelings that God is in nature and in the heart. The religious man need accept no revelation and no other authority but his own senses, heart, and understanding; and the virtuous man is one in whom conscience, developed in the social state from his inherent love of order, takes precedence over egoism, or the satisfaction of selfish wants.

The Social Contract, though primarily a work of political theory, is also a treatise on morals. Law, or the principle of order in society, lifts us from the liberty we suffer in nature to the state of freedom in which we obey the laws we prescribe for ourselves. Freedom, unlike natural liberty, is a moral condition in which the general will is the standard of individual perfection.

SOURCE. Jean Jacques Rousseau, *Profession of Faith of a Savoyard Vicar,* translated by Olive Schreiner. New York: Peter Eckler, 1889.

Thus freedom is necessity, for if perfect freedom is perfect knowledge of the good, no one would wish for anything else except through moral ignorance, or out of perversity. It is in this context that a man may be forced to be free; that is forced to conform to the laws for his own good, which coincides with that of society.

The translation of the Profession of Faith of a Savoyard Vicar *is by Olive Schreiner (N.Y., Peter Eckler, 1889), and* The Social Contract *by an anonymous translator (Dublin, William Jones, 1791).*

PROFESSION OF
FAITH OF A SAVOYARD VICAR

Introduction

... This honest ecclesiastic was a poor Savoyard, who having in his younger days incurred the displeasure of his bishop, was obliged to pass the mountains in order to seek that provision which was denied him in his own country. He was neither deficient in literature nor understanding; his talents, therefore, joined with an engaging appearance, soon procured him a patron, who recommended him as tutor to a young man of quality. He preferred poverty, however, to dependence; and being a stranger to the manners and behavior of the great, he remained but a short time in that situation. In quitting this service, however, he fortunately did not lose the esteem of his friend; and as he behaved with great prudence and was universally beloved, he flattered himself that he should in time regain the good opinion of his bishop also, and be rewarded with some little benefice in the mountains, where he hoped to spend in tranquillity and peace the remainder of his days. This was the height of his ambition. ...

The most striking circumstance of all was to observe in the retired life of my worthy master virtue without hypocrisy and humanity without weakness. His conversation was always honest and simple, and his conduct ever conformable to his discourse. I never found him troubling himself whether the persons he assisted went constantly to vespers—whether they went frequently to confession—or fasted on certain days of the week. Nor did I ever know him to impose on them any of those conditions without which a man might perish from want, and have no hope of relief from the devout. . . .

"Believe me," said he, "our mistaken notions of things are so far from hiding our misfortunes from our view that they augment those evils by rendering trifles of importance, and making us sensible of a thousand wants which we should never have known but for our prejudices. Peace of mind consists in a contempt for everything that may disturb it. The man who gives himself the greatest concern about life is he who enjoys it least; and he who aspires the most earnestly after happiness is always the one who is the most miserable."

"Alas!" cried I, with all the bitterness of discontent, "what a deplorable picture do you present of human life! If we may indulge ourselves in nothing, to what purpose were we born? If we must despise even happiness itself, who is there that can know what it is to be happy?"

"I know," replied the good priest, in a tone and manner that struck me.

"You!" said I, "so little favored by fortune! so poor! exiled! persecuted! can you be happy? And if you are, what have you done to purchase happiness?"

"My dear child," he replied, embracing me, "I will willingly tell you. As you have freely confessed to me, I will do the same to you. I will disclose to you all the sentiments of my heart. You shall see me, if not such as I really am, at least such as I believe myself to be: and when you have heard my whole *Profession of Faith*—when you know fully the situation of my heart—you will know why I think myself happy; and if you agree with me, what course you should pursue in order to become so likewise. . . ."

As I expressed an earnest desire for such an opportunity, an appointment was made for the next morning. We rose at the break of day and prepared for the journey. Leaving the town, he led me to the top of a hill, at the foot of which ran the river Po, watering in its course the fertile vales. That immense chain of mountains called the Alps terminated the distant view. The rising sun cast its welcome rays over the gilded plains, and by projecting the long shadows of the trees, the houses, and adjacent hills, formed the most beautiful scene ever mortal eye beheld. One might have been almost tempted to think that nature had at this moment displayed all its grandeur and beauty as a subject for our conversation. Here it was that, after contemplating for a short time the surrounding objects in silence, my teacher and benefactor confided to me with impressive earnestness the principles and faith which governed his life and conduct.

Profession of Faith of a Savoyard Vicar

. . . I was in that state of doubt and uncertainty in which Descartes requires the mind to be involved in order to enable it to investigate truth. This disposition of mind, however, is too disquieting to long continue, its duration being owing only to indolence or vice. My heart was not so corrupt as to seek fresh indulgence; and nothing preserves so well the habit of reflection as to be more content with ourselves than with our fortune.

I reflected, therefore, on the unhappy lot of mortals floating always on the ocean of human opinions, without compass or rudder—left to the mercy of their tempestuous passions, with no other guide than an inexperienced pilot, ignorant of his course, as well as from whence he came, and whither he is going. I often said to myself: I love the truth—I seek, yet cannot find it. Let anyone show it to me and I will readily embrace it. Why doth it hide its charms from a heart formed to adore them?

I have frequently experienced at times much greater evils; and yet no part of my life was ever so constantly disagreeable to me as that interval of scruples and anxiety. Running perpetually from one doubt and uncertainty to another, all that I could deduce from my long and painful meditations was incertitude, obscurity, and contradiction, as well with regard to my existence as to my duty.

I cannot comprehend how any man can be sincerely a skeptic on principle. Such philosophers either do not exist, or they are certainly the most miserable of men. To be in doubt about things which it is important for us to know is a situation too perplexing for the human mind; it cannot long support such incertitude; but will, in spite of itself, determine one way or the other, rather deceiving itself than being content to believe nothing of the matter.

What added further to my perplexity was that, as the authority of the church in which I was educated was decisive, and tolerated not the slightest doubt, in rejecting one point, I thereby rejected in a manner all the others. The impossibility of admitting so many absurd decisions threw doubt over those more reasonable. In being told I must believe all I was prevented from believing anything, and I knew not what course to pursue.

In this situation I consulted the philosophers. I turned over their books, and examined their several opinions. I found them vain, dogmatical, and dictatorial—even in their pretended skepticism. Ignorant of nothing, yet proving nothing; but ridiculing one another instead; and in this last particular only, in which they were all agreed, they seemed to be in the right. Affecting to triumph whenever they attacked their opponents, they lacked everything to make them capable of a vigorous defense. If you examine their reasons, you will find them calculated only to refute: If you number voices, everyone is reduced to his own suffrage. They agree in nothing but in disputing, and to attend to these was certainly not the way to remove my uncertainty. . . .

I could further see that, instead of clearing up any unnecessary doubts, the philosophers only contributed to multiply those which most tormented me, and that they resolved absolutely none. I therefore applied to another guide, and said to myself, let me consult my innate instructor, who will deceive me less than I may be deceived by others; or at least the errors I fall into will be my own, and I shall grow less depraved in the pursuit of my own illusions than in giving myself up to the deceptions of others. . . .

The love of truth then comprises all my philosophy; and my method of research being the simple and easy rule of common sense, which dispenses with the vain subtlety of argumentation, I re-examined by this principle all the knowledge of which I was possessed, resolved to admit as evident everything to which I could not in the sincerity of my heart refuse to assent, to admit also as true all that seemed to have a necessary connection with it, and to leave everything else as uncertain, without either rejecting or admitting, being determined not to trouble myself about clearing up any point which did not tend to utility in practice. . . .

To perceive is only to feel or be sensible of things; to compare them is to judge of their existence. To judge of things and to be sensible of them are very different. Things present themselves to our sensations as single and detached from each other, such as they barely exist in nature; but in our intellectual comparison of them they are removed, transported as it were, from place to place, disposed on and beside each other, to enable us to pronounce concerning their difference and similitude. The characteristic faculty of an intelligent, active being is, in my opinion, that of giving a sense to the word "exist." In beings merely sensitive, I have searched in vain to discover the like force of intellect; nor can I conceive it to be in their nature. Such passive beings present themselves; they are perceived as united into one. Such beings having no power to place one in competition with, beside, or upon the other, they cannot compare them, or judge of their separate existence. . . .

I am not, therefore, a mere sensitive and passive, but an active and intelligent, being; and whatever philosophers may pretend, lay claim to the honor of thinking. I know only that truth depends on the existence of things, and not on my understanding which judges of them; and that the less such judgment depends on me, the nearer I am certain of approaching the truth. Hence my rule of confiding more on sentiment than reason is confirmed by reason itself. . . .

You will ask me if the motions of animals are spontaneous. I will freely answer: I cannot positively tell, but analogy speaks in the affirmative. You may ask me further how I know there is such a thing as spontaneous motion. I answer: Because I feel it. I *will* to move my arm, and accordingly, it moves without the intervention of any other immediate cause. It is in vain to attempt to reason me out of this sentiment; it is more powerful than any rational evidence. You might as well attempt to convince me that I do not exist. . . .

The visible universe, however, is composed of inanimate matter, which appears to have nothing in its composition of organization, or that sensation which is common to the parts of an animated body, as it is certain that we ourselves, being parts thereof, do not perceive our existence in the whole. The universe, also, is in motion; and its movements being all regular, uniform, and subjected to constant laws, nothing appears therein similar to that liberty which is remarkable in the spontaneous motion of men and animals. The world, therefore, is not a huge self-moving animal, but receives its motions from some foreign cause, which we do not perceive; but I am so strongly persuaded within myself of the existence of this cause that it is impossible for me to observe the apparent diurnal revolution of the sun without conceiving that some force must urge it forward; or if it is the earth itself that turns, I cannot but conceive that some hand must turn it. . . .

If from matter being put in motion I discover the existence of a *will* as the first active cause, the subjugation of this matter to certain regular laws of motion displays also intelligence. This is my second article of faith. To act, to compare, to prefer, are the operations of an active, thinking being: such a being, therefore, exists. Do you proceed to ask me where I discover its existence. I answer: Not only in the revolutions of the celestial bodies; not only in myself; but in the flocks that feed on the plain, in the birds that fly in the air, in the stone that falls to the ground, and in the leaf that trembles in the wind. . . .

In meditating on the nature of man, I conceived that I discovered two distinct principles; the one raising him to the study of eternal truth, the love of justice and moral beauty—bearing him aloft to the regions of the intellectual world, the contemplation of which yields the truest delight to the philosopher—the other debasing him even below himself, subjecting him to the slavery of sense, the tyranny of the passions, and exciting these to counteract every noble and generous sentiment inspired by the former. When I perceived myself hurried away by two such contrary powers, I naturally concluded that man is not one simple and individual substance. I will, and I will not; I perceive myself at once free and a slave; I see what is good, I admire it, and yet I do the evil: I am active when I listen to my reason, and passive when hurried away by my passions; while my greatest uneasiness is to find, when fallen under temptations, that I had the power of resisting them. . . .

No material being can be self-active, and I perceive that I am so. It is in vain to dispute with me so clear a point. My own sentiment carries with it a stronger conviction than any reason which can ever be brought against it. I have a body on which other bodies act, and which acts reciprocally upon them. This reciprocal action is indubitable; but my will is independent of my senses. I can either consent to, or resist, their impressions. I am either vanquished or victor, and perceive clearly within myself when I act according to my will, and when I submit to be gov-

erned by my passions. I have always the power to will, though not
the force to execute it. When I give myself up to any temptation,
I act from the impulse of external objects. When I reproach myself for my weakness in so doing, I listen only to the dictates of
my will. I am a slave in my vices, and free in my repentance. The
sentiment of my liberty is effaced only by my depravation, and
when I prevent the voice of the soul from being heard in opposition to the laws of the body. . . .

If man be an active and free being, he acts of himself. None of
his spontaneous actions, therefore, enter into the general system
of Providence, nor can be imputed to it. Providence doth not con-
trive the evil, which is the consequence of man's abusing the
liberty his Creator gave him; it only doth not prevent it, either
because the evil which so impotent a being is capable of doing is
beneath its notice, or because it cannot prevent it without laying
a restraint upon his liberty, and causing a greater evil by debasing
his nature. Providence hath left man at liberty, not that he should
do evil, but good, by choice. . . .

Inquire no longer then, who is the author of evil. Behold him
in yourself. There exists no other evil in nature than what you
either do or suffer, and you are equally the author of both. A
general evil could exist only in disorder, but in the system of
nature I see an established order, which is never disturbed. Particular evil exists only in the sentiment of the suffering being;
and this sentiment is not given to man by nature, but is of his
own acquisition. Pain and sorrow have but little hold on those
who, unaccustomed to reflection, have neither memory nor foresight. Take away our fatal improvements—take away our errors
and our vices—take away, in short, everything that is the work
of man, and all that remains is good. . . .

After having thus deduced this most important truth, from the
impressions of perceptible objects and that innate principle which
leads me to judge of natural causes from experience, it remains
for me to inquire what maxims I ought to draw therefrom for my
conduct in life—what rules I ought to prescribe to myself in order
to fulfill my destiny on earth agreeably to the design of Him who
placed me here. To pursue my own method, I deduce these rules
not from the sublime principles of philosophy, but find them
written in indelible characters on my heart. I have only to consult
myself concerning what I ought to do. All that I feel to be right,

is right; whatever I feel to be wrong, is wrong. Conscience is the ablest of all casuists, and it is only when we are trafficking with her that we have recourse to the subtleties of logical ratiocination. . . . Reason deceives us but too often, and has given us a right to distrust her conclusions; but conscience never deceives us. She is to the soul what instinct is to the body—she is man's truest and safest guide. Whoever puts himself under the conduct of this guide pursues the direct path of nature, and need not fear to be misled. This point is very important (pursued my benefactor, perceiving I was going to interrupt him); permit me to detain you a little longer in order to clear it up. . . .

There evidently exists, then, in the soul of man, an innate principle of justice and goodness, by which, in spite of our own maxims, we approve or condemn the actions of ourselves and others. To this principle it is that I give the appellation of conscience. . . .

To know what is virtuous is not to love virtue. Man has no innate knowledge of virtue; but no sooner is it made known to him by reason than conscience induces him to love and admire it. This is the innate sentiment I mean. . . .

Ah! let us not spoil the man of nature, and he will always be virtuous without constraint, and happy without remorse.

. . .

Thus, my young friend, have I given you with my own lips a recital of my creed, such as the Supreme Being reads it in my heart. You are the first person to whom I have made this *Profession of Faith;* and you are the only one, probably, to whom I shall ever make it. . . .

Adopt only those of my sentiments which you believe are true, and reject all the others; and whatever religion you may ultimately embrace, remember that its real duties are independent of human institutions—that no religion upon earth can dispense with the sacred obligations of morality—that an upright heart is the temple of the Divinity—and that, in every country and in every sect, to love God above all things, and thy neighbor as thyself, is the substance and summary of the law—the end and aim of religious duty.

THE SOCIAL CONTRACT

Book One

My design in this treatise is to enquire whether, taking men such as they are, and laws such as they may be made, it is not possible to establish some just and certain rule for the administration of a free state.

CHAPTER I

Subject of the First Book. Man is born free, and yet we see him everywhere in chains: and those who believe themselves the masters of others cease not to be even greater slaves than the people they govern. How this happens I am ignorant; but if I am asked what renders it legal, I believe it may be in my power to resolve the question.

If I were only to consider force, and the effects of it, I should say that when a nation is constrained to obey, and does obey, it does well; but whenever it can throw off its yoke, and does throw it off, it does better. The people may certainly use for the recovery of their liberty, the same means that were employed to deprive them of it; it was either intended to be recovered, or not to be torn from them.

The social order is a sacred right which serves for the basis of all others: yet this right comes not from nature; it is founded on conventions. The question is what those conventions are. But, before I come to the point, I must establish the principles which I intend to proceed upon. . . .

CHAPTER III

Of the Right of the Strongest. The strongest are still never sufficiently strong to insure them the continual mastership, unless they find means of transforming force into right, and obedience into duty.

From the right of the strongest, right takes an ironical appearance, and is rarely established as a principle. But how shall we explain the term? Force is a physical power, and I do not see what

SOURCE. Rousseau, *The Social Contract.* Dublin: William Jones, 1791.

morality can result from its effects. To yield to force is an act of necessity, not of inclination; or it is at best only an act of prudence. In what sense then can it be an act of duty?

Let us suppose for a moment the existence of this pretended right. I see nothing that can arise from it but inexplicable nonsense; for if we admit that force constitutes right, the effect changes with the cause; and all force which overcomes the former possessor succeeds to its right: as soon as men can disobey with impunity, they can lawfully; and because the strongest has always reason on his side, strength is the only thing men should seek to acquire. But what sort of a right is that which perishes with the force that gave it existence? If it is necessary to obey by force, there can be no occasion to obey from duty; and when force is no more, all obligation ceases with it: so that this right of the strongest adds nothing to the right of force, but is indeed an unmeaning term.

If in saying *let us obey the powerful,* they mean to say *let us yield to force,* the precept is good, but it is superfluous, for it never is or can be violated.

All power, we are told, comes from God. I grant it does; but all diseases likewise come from the same Hand, and yet who ever forbid us to call in a physician? If a robber surprises me in a dark recess of a wood, it is necessary that I should give him my purse when forced to do so; but am I in conscience obliged to give it to him, though I should be in a situation to subdue or escape from him? The fact is, the pistol which he holds is his power.

We must grant, therefore, that force does not constitute right, and that obedience is only due to the legitimate powers. Thus everything refers to my first question.

. . .

CHAPTER VI

Of the Social Contract. We will suppose that men in a state of nature are arrived at that crisis when the strength of each individual is insufficient to defend him from the attacks he is subject to. This primitive state can therefore subsist no longer; and the human race must perish, unless they change their manner of life.

As men cannot create for themselves new forces, but merely

unite and direct those which already exist, the only means they can employ for their preservation is to form by aggregation an assemblage of forces that may be able to resist all assaults, be put in motion as one body, and act in concert upon all occasions.

This assemblage of forces must be produced by the concurrence of many; and as the force and the liberty of a man are the chief instruments of his preservation, how can he engage them without danger, and without neglecting the care which is due to himself? This doubt, which leads directly to my subject, may be expressed in these words:

"Where shall we find a form of association which will defend and protect with the whole aggregate force the person and the property of each individual; and by which every person, while united with ALL, shall obey only HIMSELF, and remain as free as before the union?" Such is the fundamental problem, of which the social contract gives the solution.

The articles of this contract are so unalterably fixed by the nature of the act that the least modification renders them vain and of no effect. They are the same everywhere, and are everywhere understood and admitted, even though they may never have been formally announced: so that, when once the social pact is violated in any instance, all the obligations it created cease; and each individual is restored to his original rights, and resumes his native liberty, as the consequence of losing that conventional liberty for which he exchanged them.

All the articles of the social contract will, when clearly understood, be found reducible to this single point—THE TOTAL ALIENATION OF EACH ASSOCIATE, AND ALL HIS RIGHTS, TO THE WHOLE COMMUNITY. For every individual gives himself up entirely—the condition of every person is alike—and being so, it would not be the interest of anyone to render himself offensive to others.

Nay, more than this: the alienation is made without any reserve; the union is as complete as it can be, and no associate has a claim to anything; for if any individual was to retain rights not enjoyed in general by all, as there would be no common superior to decide between him and the public, each person, being in some points his own proper judge, would soon pretend to be so in everything; and thus would the state of nature be revived, and the association become tyrannical or be annihilated.

In fine, each person gives himself to ALL, but not to any INDIVIDUAL: and as there is no one associate over whom the same right is not acquired which is ceded to him by others, each gains an equivalent for what he loses, and finds his force increased for preserving that which he possesses.

If, therefore, we exclude from the social compact all that is not essentially necessary, we shall find it reduced to the following terms:

"We each of us places, in common, his person, and all his power, under the supreme direction of the general will; and we receive into the body each member as an indivisible part of the whole."

From that moment, instead of so many separate persons as there are contractors, this act of association produces a moral collective body, composed of as many members as there are voices in the assembly; which from this act receives its unity, its common self, its life, and its will. This public person, which is thus formed by the union of all the private persons, took formerly the name of *city,* and now takes that of *republic* or *body politic.* It is called by its members *state* when it is passive, and *sovereign* when in activity: and whenever it is spoken of with other bodies of a similar kind, it is denominated *power.* The associates take collectively the name of *people,* and separately that of *citizens,* as participating in the sovereign authority; they are also styled *subjects,* because they are subjected to the laws. But these terms are frequently confounded, and used one for the other; and a man must understand them well to distinguish when they are properly employed.

CHAPTER VII

Of the Sovereign Power. It appears from this form that the act of association contains a reciprocal engagement between the public and individuals; and that each individual contracting, as it were with himself, is engaged under a double character; that is, as a part of the *sovereign power* engaging with individuals, and as a member of the state entering into a compact with the *sovereign power.* But we cannot apply here the maxim of civil right that no person is bound by an engagement which he makes with himself; for there is a material difference between an obligation contracted toward *oneself* individually, and toward a collective body of which *oneself* constitutes a part. . . .

As soon as the multitude is thus united in one body, you cannot offend one of its members without attacking the whole, without incurring the resentment of all the members. Thus duty and interest equally oblige the two contracting parties to lend their mutual aid to each other; and the same men must endeavor to unite under this double character all the advantages which attend it.

The sovereign power, being formed only of the individuals which compose it, neither has, nor can have, any interest contrary to theirs; consequently, the sovereign power requires no guarantee toward its subjects, because it is impossible that the body should seek to injure all its members: and we shall see presently that it can do no injury to any individual. The sovereign power, by its nature, must, while it exists, be everything it ought to be: but it is not so with subjects toward the sovereign power; to which, notwithstanding the common interest subsisting between them, there is nothing to answer for the performance of their engagements if some means is not found of insuring their fidelity.

In fact, each individual may, as a man, have a private will, dissimilar or contrary to the general will which he has as a citizen. His own particular interest may dictate to him very differently from the common interest; his mind, naturally and absolutely independent, may regard what he owes to the common cause as a gratuitous contribution, the omission of which would be less injurious to others than the payment would be burdensome to himself; and considering the moral person which constitutes the state as a creature of the imagination, because it is not a man, he may wish to enjoy the rights of a citizen without being disposed to fulfill the duties of a subject: an injustice which would in its progress cause the ruin of the body politic.

In order therefore to prevent the social compact from becoming a vain form, it tacitly comprehends this engagement, which alone can give effect to the others: that whoever refuses to obey the general will shall be compelled to it by the whole body, which is in fact only forcing him to be free; for this is the condition which guarantees his absolute personal independence to every citizen of the country—a condition which gives motion and effect to the political machine; which alone renders all civil engagements legal; and without which they would be absurd, tyrannical, and subject to the most enormous abuses.

CHAPTER VIII

Of the Civil State. The passing from a state of nature to a civil state produces in man a very remarkable change, by substituting justice for instinct, and giving to his actions a moral character which they wanted before.

It is at the moment of that transition that the voice of duty succeeds to physical impulse; and a sense of what is right, to the incitements of appetite. The man who had till then regarded none but himself perceives that he must act on other principles, and learns to consult his reason before he listens to his propensities.

Although he is deprived in this new state of many advantages which he enjoyed from nature, he gains others of equal consequence. His faculties unfold themselves by being exercised; his ideas are extended; his sentiments exalted; and his whole mind becomes so enlarged and refined that if, by abusing his new condition, he sometimes degrades it even below that from which he emerged, he ought still to bless, without ceasing, the happy moment that changed him from a circumscribed and stupid animal to a free intelligent being; in a word, to a man.

In order to draw a balance between the advantages and disadvantages attending his new situation, let us state them in such a manner that they may be easily compared.

A man loses by the social contract his natural liberty, and an unlimited right to all which tempts him, and which he can obtain. In return he acquires civil liberty, and a just right to all he possesses.

That we may not be deceived in the value of these compensations, we must distinguish natural liberty, which knows no bounds but the power of the individual, from civil liberty, which is limited by the general will; and that possession which is only the effect of force, or of first occupancy, from that property which must be founded on a positive title.

We may add to the other acquisitions of the civil state, that of moral liberty, which alone renders a man master of himself: for it is slavery to be under the impulse of appetite; and freedom to obey the laws. But I have already said too much on this head; and the philosophical sense of the word "liberty" is not at present my subject.

. . .

Book Two

CHAPTER III

Whether the General Will Can Err. It follows from what has been said that the general will is always right, and tends always to the public advantage; but it does not follow that the resolutions of the people have always the same rectitude. Their will always seeks the public good, but it does not always perceive how it is to be attained. The people are never corrupted, but they are often deceived; and under the influence of deception the public will may err.

There is frequently much difference between the *will of all* and the *general will*. The latter regards only the common interest; the former regards private interest, and is indeed but a collection of the wills of individuals: but remove from these the wills that oppose each other, and then the general will remains.

If, when a people sufficiently informed deliberate, there was to be no communication between them, from a great number of trifling differences the general will would always result, and their resolutions be always good. But when cabals and partial associations are formed at the expense of the public, the wills of such meetings, though *general* with regard to the agreement of their members, are *private* with regard to the state; and it can be said no longer that "there are as many voters as men," but as many as there are associations: by this means, the differences being less numerous, they produce a result less general.

In fine, when one of these associations becomes so large that it prevails over all the rest, its will domineers; and you have no longer, as the result of your public deliberations, the sum of many opinions dissenting in a small degree from each other; but that of one great dictating dissentient. From that moment there is no more a general will, but the predominating opinion is that of an individual. It is therefore of the utmost importance for obtaining the real *will of the public* that no partial associations should be formed in a state; and that every citizen should speak his opinion entirely from himself. Such was the unique and sublime instruction given by Lycurgus to the Spartans.

When there are partial associations, it is politic to multiply their number, that they may all be kept on an equality. This method was pursued by Solon, Numa, and Servius; and these are the only precautions that can be taken to make the general will always clear, and prevent the people from being deceived. . . .

CHAPTER VI

Of the Law. By the social compact we have given existence and life to the body politic; it now remains to give it motion and will for legislation. For the primitive act by which the body is formed determines none of the measures that are necessary for its preservation.

What is good, and conformable to order, is so from the nature of things, and independently of human conventions. Justice flows from God: He only is the source of it; and if men could be made sensible of its Divine authority, we should require neither government or laws. This principle of justice is also undoubtedly universal and founded on reason; but it can never, without the aid of human institutions, be sufficient for the purpose of society, unless its influence were equal on the minds of all men, and the conduct of all men equally regulated by its dictates. The natural principle of justice which would operate partially, and not be reciprocal between ALL, must be injurious to the *good,* and advantageous to the *bad,* part of mankind; for while the former invariable adhered to its rules, even to their own detriment, the latter would never restrain themselves by them. There must therefore be conventions and laws to combine our duties and our rights; to render the practice of justice mutual between man and man; and to direct it to its great end, the welfare and happiness of ALL. In a state of nature, where everything is in common, I can owe nothing to those to whom I have promised nothing; and I will not acknowledge that anything but what I do not wish to possess can be exclusively the property of another person. It is not so in a civil state, where the right of every man is determined by law. . . .

When I say that the object of the laws is always general, I mean that the law views its subjects collectively, and their actions abstractly; never regarding a man as an individual, or an action as that of a private man. Thus the law may enact that there shall be certain privileges, but it cannot name the persons who are to enjoy them. The law may divide the citizens into many classes, and specify the qualifications which shall give a right of admission to each class; but it cannot direct such or such a person to be admitted. The law can establish a royal government, and an hereditary succession; but it cannot elect a king, or appoint successors to the crown. In a word, those functions which relate to any individual pertain not to the legislative power.

Under this idea, we perceive at once how unnecessary it would be to inquire to whom belongs the function of making law; because the laws are but the acts of the general will. Neither need we ask whether the prince is above the laws; since he is a member of the state. Or, whether the law can be unjust; as nothing is unjust toward itself. It would be equally superfluous to inquire how people can be free while subjected to the laws; because the laws which they must obey are but the registers of their own wills.

We see also that the law uniting the universality of the will and that of the object, whatever is ordered by any man of his own accord is not law; nay, even that which the sovereign power orders relative to a private object is not a law, but a decree; neither is it an act of the sovereignty, but of the magistracy.

I therefore denominate every state a republic which is regulated by laws, under whatever form of administration it may be; for then only the public interest governs, and the affairs of the public obtain a due regard. All lawful governments are republican; and I will hereafter explain what that government is.

The laws are properly but the conditions of the civil association. The people submit themselves to the laws to enjoy the right of making them; and it pertains to those who associate to regulate the terms of association. But how do they regulate them? Is it by common agreement; by sudden inspiration? Has the body politic an organ for declaring its will? Who gives to that body the provident care of forming these acts, and publishing them beforehand; or how are they declared at the moment of occasion? How can an unenlightened multitude, who often, we must suppose, do not see what is immediately before their sight, since they so seldom act as they ought to do—how can they execute, of themselves, so great, so difficult an enterprise as a system of legislation?

The people are always solicitous to promote their own welfare, but of themselves they do not always know in what it consists. The general will is always right, but the judgment that guides it is not always sufficiently enlightened. It is therefore necessary to make the people see things such as they are, or sometimes such as they ought to appear; to point out to them the right path, which they are seeking for; to guard them from the seducing voice of faction; and representing to them the possible as well as the probable consequences of events, induce them to balance the attraction of immediate and sensible advantage against the apprehension of unknown and distant evil. Individuals would then pursue the good which they might otherwise have rejected, and the public would learn to anticipate advantages of which they could have only a perspective view. All men have equally occasion for guides: some to make their wills conformable to their reason, and others to teach them what it is they wish to obtain. From this increase of public knowledge would result the union of judgment and will in the social body; from that union, the harmony and uniform agreement of all parties; and from thence, the legislature.

. . .

Book Three

CHAPTER I

Of Government in General. We have seen that the legislative power belongs to the people, and can belong to that body only. It is easy to see, on the contrary, by the principles already established, that the executive power cannot belong to the body of the people, as legislator or sovereign; because that power exists only for the performance of private acts, which are not to be performed by the law, neither by the sovereign, all whose acts must be laws. It is therefore necessary that the public force should have an agent which shall unite and employ that force according to the direction of the general will—serve as the means of communication between the state and the sovereign—and form a sort of public person, in which, as in a man, the union of mind and body should be found. This is the reason why the government in a state is generally, and very improperly, confounded with the sovereign power, of which it is but the minister.

Thus we see that government is an intermedial power established between the subjects and the sovereign, for their mutual correspondence; and charged with the execution of the laws, and the maintenance of civil and political liberty. . . .

There is this essential difference between the state and the government; the former is self-existent, and the existence of the latter depends entirely on the sovereign power—so that the ruling will of the prince (the government) is or ought to be nothing more than the general will, or the law; and its power, only the public power, concentrated in its hands, which if it attempts to assume to itself by any absolute and independent act, the chain which combined the whole relaxes immediately. And if at last the private will of the prince is more active in the direction of affairs than the will of the sovereign; and the power delegated to the prince by the sovereign is employed to enforce obedience to such private will, so that there are in effect two sovereigns, the one by right, and the other in fact; at that moment the social union ceases, and the body politic is dissolved. . . .

The great difficulty of forming a body of government lies in ordering the chain of subaltern arrangements in such a manner that the general constitution may not be altered by giving too much strength to any part; but that the power necessary for preserving the body may be kept subordinate to, and distinct from, that which is necessary to preserve the state; and, in fine, that on every occasion the government may be sacrificed to the people, and not the people to the government.

. . .

Book Four

CHAPTER I

That the General Will Cannot Be Destroyed. If you unite many men, and consider them as one body, they will have but one will; and that will must be to promote the common safety and general well-being of all.

While this union of men and of mind continues, all the springs of the political machine will be vigorous and unembarrassed; the maxims by which they are regulated will be wise and comprehensible; and there will be no jarring interests to destroy the general harmony by creating discord amongst the parts. The common good of all will then be the grand object of attention; the means of pursuing it will be evident; and nothing necessary but a sound understanding to perceive in what that good consists: for peace, union, and equality are enemies to subtle politics; and men of purity and integrity are, from their attachment to what is plain and honest, not easily led astray by the lures and deceptions of deep politicians; in a word, they have not cunning enough to be dupes. Men of this description despise, as all men ought to do, the refinements of those nations which are rendered miserable by so much art and mystery.

That these two characteristics of politicians are not only often injurious, but always unnecessary, may be proved by the example of the happiest people in the world; amongst whom a company of peasants, sitting under the shade of an oak, conduct the affairs of the nation with a degree of wisdom and equity that do honor to human nature.

A state thus governed by chiefs who disdain the dark refinements of policy requires but very few laws; and whenever it becomes necessary to promulgate new ones, the necessity is perceived universally; and he who proposes them does only what every other citizen knows to be expedient: of course, neither eloquence or address is required to obtain the general concurrence in a measure which each person had already resolved to adopt, as soon as he should find his fellow citizens convinced as well as himself of its utility. . . .

When the social bond once begins to relax, when private interest takes the lead in public affairs, and small associations have an influence on the resolves of the people, the general interest of the state finds many opposers; and the general will, now destitute of unanimity, is no longer the will of all, but everything is contested, and the best advice never adopted without much dispute and opposition.

In fine, when a state upon the brink of ruin supports only a vain illusive form, and the social bond no longer unites the hearts of the people; and when the sacred name of public good is made use of to cover the basest views of private interest; then the general will is silenced, and everything being directed by secret influence, the citizens give their suffrages no more than if the state had never existed. Decrees of the most iniquitous tendency are then passed, to which the name of laws is falsely given, and everything concurs in promoting the triumph of despotism over an unhappy nation.

But it does not follow that the general will is annihilated, or yet corrupted: that will remains always constant, unalterable, and pure; but it is rendered subordinate to other wills, which domineer over, and keep it mute. . . .

CHAPTER VIII

Of Civil Religion. . . . It is of consequence to the state that each of its citizens should be of such a religion as will dispose him to perform his duties: but the dogmas of that religion interest neither the state, nor the members of the state; except as far as they affect morality, and those duties which the professor of it is required to discharge toward others. Every individual may, while he does not suffer his religious tenets to lead him into any action, or any omission, which may be injurious to others, entertain what opinions he please, without being controlled in them by the sovereign; who, having no jurisdiction in the other world has no concern with the situation of men in a future life, provided they are good citizens in the present one.

There is, however, a profession of faith merely civil, the articles of which it is the business of the sovereign to arrange; not precisely as dogmas of religion, but as sentiments conducive to the well-being of society; and without which, it is impossible to be either a good citizen or a faithful subject.

The sovereign has no power by which he can oblige men to believe the articles of faith which are thus laid down: but the unbeliever may be banished from the state; not as an impious person, but as one unfit for that society; because incapable, from his principles, of being sincerely attached to equity and the laws; or of sacrificing, if occasion should require it, his life to his duty as a citizen. But if anyone, after he has subscribed to these dogmas, shall conduct himself as if he did not believe them, he may be punished with death: for he has committed the greatest of all crimes, he has lied in the face of the law.

The articles of the civil creed must be simple, few in number, precisely fixed, and free from either explanations or comment. The points insisted on must be: a belief in one God, powerful, wise, and benevolent; who beholds all, and provides for all; an expectation of a future life, where the just will be rewarded, and the wicked punished; and a firm confidence in the sanctity of the social contract, and the laws. The renunciations of this creed I would confine to one single object—I mean intolerance, whose spirit is only congenial to the religions I would exclude.

Those who make a distinction between civil and religious intolerance are certainly, in my opinion, mistaken; for they must be inseparable; for it is impossible to live in amity with those whom we believe devoted to damnation: to love them would be to insult that God who has marked them for the objects of His wrath. We should either reclaim or punish them.

Religious intolerance is admitted everywhere, and it is impossible for it not to produce some civil effect; as soon as it has produced it, the sovereign ceases to be such, even in temporal concerns; for the priests are from that time so absolutely masters that kings themselves are nothing more than their officers.

Now that there neither is, or can be any more, an exclusive national religion, all religions ought to be tolerated whose tenets discover nothing contradictory to the duties of a citizen; but those who dare to say *Out of the church, out of salvation* should be driven from the state, unless that state is the church, and the prince the pontiff. Such a dogma is only suited to a religious government; in all others it must be exceedingly pernicious. The very reason which it is said made Henry IV embrace the Romish religion is the one which should make all honest men renounce it; and particularly all princes, who are capable of reasoning as they ought to do.

2   *Condorcet*

Marie Jean Antoine Nicolas Caritat, Marquis de Condorcet (1743–1794), was born of an old noble family, and became a mathematician of note. He was elected to the Legislative Assembly during the French Revolution, but fell from favor during the Terror and died in prison (most likely by suicide).

Condorcet's Sketch for a Historical Picture of the Progress of the Human Mind, written while in hiding from the authorities, is a major document in the history of the idea of progress. It does not speak of necessary perfection, as some later philosophies did, but of perfectibility, or the capacity in man for earthly perfection. Condorcet argued that the discovery of the laws of social phenomena might one day free man from want and from the fear of war, which so largely condition his behavior. In this case, all that is needed to produce peace and well-being on earth is to educate man; he will then act to better his condition. Education has always been central to the liberal creed which the philosophes represented, indeed, helped to create.

Condorcet's work sets forth with clarity and precision the essential meaning of science as it was understood by the philosophes: that it is a way of thinking useful to man in the avoidance of prejudice, dogmatism, and intolerance, and which works to enhance the dignity of the individual while it raises the intellectual and material level of humanity as a whole. These are the humanistic as well as humanitarian goals, each necessary to the other, that characterize the Age of Enlightenment.

The following translation is by June Barraclough (N.Y., The Noonday Press, 1955).

SOURCE. Condorcet, *Sketch for a Historical Picture of the Progress of the Mind,* tr. by June Barraclough, New York Noonday Press, 1955. Reprinted by permission of Humanities Press Inc. and George Weidenfeld & Nicolson Ltd.

SKETCH FOR A HISTORICAL PICTURE
OF THE PROGRESS OF THE HUMAN MIND

Introduction

Man is born with the ability to receive sensations; to perceive them and to distinguish between the various simple sensations of which they are composed; to remember, recognize, and combine them; to compare these combinations; to apprehend what they have in common and the ways in which they differ; to attach signs to them all in order to recognize them more easily and to allow for the ready production of new combinations.

This faculty is developed in him through the action of external objects, that is to say, by the occurrence of certain composite sensations whose constancy or coherence in change are independent of him; through communication with other beings like himself; and finally, through various artificial methods which these first developments have led him to invent.

Sensations are attended by pleasure or pain; and man for his part has the capacity to transform such momentary impressions into permanent feelings of an agreeable or disagreeable character, and then to experience these feelings when he either observes or recollects the pleasures and pains of other sentient beings.

Finally, as a consequence of this capacity and of his ability to form and combine ideas, there arise between him and his fellow creatures ties of interest and duty, to which nature herself has wished to attach the most precious portion of our happiness and the most painful of our ills.

If one confines oneself to the study and observation of the general facts and laws about the development of these faculties, considering only what is common to all human beings, this science is called metaphysics. But if one studies this development as it manifests itself in the inhabitants of a certain area at a certain period of time and then traces it on from generation to generation, one has the picture of the progress of the human mind. This progress is subject to the same general laws that can be observed in the development of the faculties of the individual, and it is indeed no more than the sum of that development realized in a large number of individuals joined together in society. What happens at any particular moment is the result of what has happened at all previous moments, and itself has an influence on what will happen in the future.

So such a picture is historical, since it is a record of change and is based on the observation of human societies throughout the different stages of their development. It ought to reveal the order of this change and the influence that each moment exerts upon the subsequent moment, and so ought also to show, in the modifications that the human species has undergone, ceaselessly renewing itself through the immensity of the centuries, the path that it has followed, the steps that it has made toward truth or happiness.

Such observations upon what man has been, and what he is today, will instruct us about the means we should employ to make certain and rapid the further progress that his nature allows him still to hope for.

Such is the aim of the work that I have undertaken, and its result will be to show by appeal to reason and fact that nature has set no term to the perfection of human faculties; that the perfectibility of man is truly indefinite; and that the progress of this perfectibility, from now onward, independent of any power that might wish to halt it, has no other limit than the duration of the globe upon which nature has cast us. This progress will doubtless vary in speed, but it will never be reversed as long as the earth occupies its present place in the system of the universe, and as long as the general laws of this system produce neither a general cataclysm nor such changes as will deprive the human race of its present faculties and its present resources. . . .

The Eighth Stage

FROM THE INVENTION OF PRINTING TO THE TIME WHEN
PHILOSOPHY AND THE SCIENCES SHOOK OFF THE YOKE
OF AUTHORITY

. . . There are two other events which took place almost at the same time as the invention of printing, of which one exerted an immediate influence over the progress of the human mind, whereas the influence of the other will be felt as long as the human race endures. I speak of the capture of Constantinople by the Turks, and the discovery of the New World and of the route that opened direct communication between Europe and the eastern parts of Africa and Asia. . . .

Intrepid men, inspired by love of glory and passion for discovery, had pushed back further the bounds of the universe for Europe, had shown her new skies and opened up unknown lands. Da Gama had reached India after following the long African coastline with unwearying patience, whilst Columbus, abandoning himself to the waves of the Atlantic Ocean, had discovered that hitherto unknown world which lies to the west of Europe and to the east of Asia. . . .

For the first time man knew the globe that he inhabited, was able to study in all countries the human race as modified by the long influence of natural causes or social institutions, and could observe the products of the earth or of the sea, in all temperatures and all climates. The wealth of every kind which these natural resources offer to men, and which is so far from being exhausted that its vast extent is as yet not even suspected; a knowledge of the natural world that can furnish new truths and destroy accredited errors in the sciences; the increased activity of trade which has given new wings to industry and navigation, and by a necessary chain of influence, to all the sciences and to all the arts; and the strength which this activity has given to free nations to resist tyrants, to enslaved peoples to break their chains or at least to relax the chains of feudalism: all these are also to be numbered amongst the fortunate consequences of these discoveries. But these discoveries will have repaid humanity what they have cost it only when Europe renounces her oppressive and avaricious system of monopoly; only when she remembers that men of all races are equally brothers by the wish of nature and have not been created to feed the vanity and greed of a few privileged nations; only when she calls upon all people to share her independence, freedom, and knowledge, which she will do once she is alive to her own true interests. Unfortunately we must still ask ourselves if this revolution will be the honorable fruit of the progress of philosophy or only, as it has hitherto been, the shameful consequence of national jealousies and the excesses of tyranny. . . .

Three great men have marked the transition from this stage of history to the next: Bacon, Galileo, Descartes.

Bacon revealed the true method of studying nature and of

using the three instruments that she has given us for penetrating
her secrets: observation, experience, and calculation. He asked
that the philosopher, cast into the middle of the universe, should
begin by renouncing all the beliefs that he had received and even
all the notions he had formed, so that he might then re-create for
himself, as it were, a new understanding admitting only of precise
ideas, accurate notions, and truths whose degree of certainty or
probability had been strictly weighed. But Bacon, who possessed
the genius of philosophy in the highest degree, was without the
genius of science; and these methods for discovering truth, of
which he gave no examples, were admired by philosophers but in
no way influenced the course of science.

Galileo enriched the sciences by useful and brilliant discoveries.
He showed by example how to arrive at knowledge of the laws of
nature by a sure and fruitful method, which did not necessitate
sacrificing the hope of success to the fear of error. He founded the
first school in which the sciences were studied without any admix-
ture of superstition in favor of either popular prejudices or authority, and where all methods other than experiment and
calculation were rejected with philosophical severity. But in
limiting himself exclusively to the mathematical and physical
sciences, he could not afford mankind that general guidance of
which it seemed to stand in need.

This honor was reserved for Descartes, a bold and clever philosopher. Endowed with great genius for the sciences, he joined
example to precept and gave a method for finding and recognizing truth. He showed how to apply this in his discovery of the
laws of dioptrics and the laws of the collision of bodies and
finally in the development of a new branch of mathematics which
was to move forward the frontiers of the subject.

He wished to extend his method to all the subjects of human
thought; God, man, and the universe were in turn the objects of
his meditations. If his progress in the physical sciences was less
certain than Galileo's, if his philosophy was less wise than
Bacon's, if he can be reproached with not having learned sufficiently from the precepts of the one and the practice of the
other, to distrust his imagination, to ask questions of nature only
by experiment, to believe only in calculation and the observation
of the universe instead of fashioning it, to study man instead of
speculating about him, still the very audacity of his mistakes

served to further the progress of the human race. He stimulated men's minds, and this all the wisdom of his rivals had never done. He commanded men to shake off the yoke of authority, to recognize none save that which was avowed by reason; and he was obeyed, because he won men by his boldness and led them by his enthusiasm.

The human mind was not yet free, but it knew that it was formed to be so. Those who dared to insist that it should be kept in its old chains or to try and impose new ones upon it were forced to show why it should submit to them; and from that day onward it was certain that they would soon be broken. . . .

The Ninth Stage

FROM DESCARTES TO THE FOUNDATION OF THE FRENCH REPUBLIC

. . . After long periods of error, after being led astray by vague or incomplete theories, publicists have at last discovered the true rights of man and how they can all be deducted from the single truth that *man is a sentient being, capable of reasoning and of acquiring moral ideas.*

They have seen that the maintenance of these rights was the sole object of men's coming together in political societies, and that the social art is the art of guaranteeing the preservation of these rights and their distribution in the most equal fashion over the largest area. It was felt that in every society the means of assuring the rights of the individual should be submitted to certain common rules, but that the authority to choose these means and to determine these rules could belong only to the majority of the members of the society itself; for in making this choice the individual cannot follow his own reason without subjecting others to it, and the will of the majority is the only mark of truth that can be accepted by all without loss of equality.

. . .

These principles, which the noble Sydney paid for with his blood and on which Locke set the authority of his name, were later developed by Rousseau with greater precision, breadth, and energy and he deserves renown for having established them among the truths that it is no longer permissible to forget or to combat. Man has certain needs and also certain faculties with which to satisfy them; from these faculties and from their products, modified and distributed in different ways, there results an accumulation of wealth out of which must be met the common needs of mankind. But what are the laws according to which this wealth is produced or distributed, accumulated or consumed, increased or dissipated? What, too, are the laws governing that general tendency toward an equilibrium between supply and demand from which it follows that, with any increase in wealth, life becomes easier and men are happier, until a point is reached when no further increase is possible; or that, again, with any decrease in wealth, life becomes harder, suffering increases, until the consequent fall in population restores the balance? How, with all the astonishing multifariousness of labor and production, supply and demand, with all the frightening complexity of conflicting interests that link the survival and well-being of one individual to the general organization of societies, that make his well-being dependent on every accident of nature and every political event, his pain and pleasure on what is happening in the remotest corner of the globe, how, with all this seeming chaos, is it that, by a universal moral law, the efforts made by each individual on his own behalf minister to the welfare of all, and that the interests of society demand that everyone should understand where his own interests lie, and should be able to follow them without hindrance?

Men, therefore, should be able to use their faculties, dispose of their wealth, and provide for their needs in complete freedom. The common interest of any society, far from demanding that they should restrain such activity, on the contrary, forbids any interference with it; and as far as this aspect of public order is concerned, the guaranteeing to each man his natural rights is at once the whole of social utility, the sole duty of the social power, the only right that the general will can legitimately exercise over the individual. . . .

Up till now we have shown the progress of philosophy only in the men who have cultivated, deepened, and perfected it. It remains for us to show what have been its effects on public opinion; how reason, while it learned to safeguard itself against the errors into which the imagination and respect for authority had so often led it, at last found a sure method of discovering and recognizing truth; and how at the same time it destroyed the prejudices of the masses which had for so long afflicted and corrupted the human race.

At last man could proclaim aloud his right, which for so long had been ignored, to submit all opinions to his own reason and to use in the search for truth the only instrument for its recognition that he has been given. Every man learned with a sort of pride that nature had not forever condemned him to base his beliefs on the opinions of others; the superstitions of supernatural religion disappeared from society as from philosophy.

Soon there was formed in Europe a class of men who were concerned less with the discovery or development of the truth than with its propagation, men who whilst devoting themselves to the tracking down of prejudices in the hiding places where the priests, the schools, the governments, and all long-established institutions had gathered and protected them, made it their lifework to destroy popular errors rather than to drive back the frontiers of human knowledge—an indirect way of aiding its progress which was not less fraught with peril, nor less useful.

In England, Collins and Bolingbroke, in France, Bayle, Fontenelle, Voltaire, Montesquieu, and the schools founded by these famous men, fought on the side of truth, using in turn all the weapons with which learning, philosophy, wit, and literary talent can furnish reason; using every mood from humor to pathos, every literary form from the vast erudite encyclopedia to the novel or the broadsheet of the day; covering truth with a veil that spared weaker eyes and excited one to guess what lay beyond it; skillfully flattering prejudices so as to attack them the better; seldom threatening them, and then always either only one in its entirety or several partially; sometimes conciliating the enemies of reason by seeming to wish only for a half tolerance in religious matters, only for a half freedom in politics; sparing despotism when tilting against the absurdities of religion, and religion when abusing tyranny; yet always attacking the principles of these two scourges even when they seemed to be against only their more revolting or ridiculous abuses, and laying their axes to the very roots of these sinister threes when they appeared to be lopping off a few stray branches; sometimes teaching the friends of liberty that superstition is the invincible shield behind which despotism shelters and should therefore be the first victim to be sacrificed, the first chain to be broken, and sometimes denouncing it to the

despots as the real enemy of their power, and frightening them
with stories of its secret machinations and its bloody persecutions; never ceasing to demand the independence of reason and
the freedom of the press as the right and the salvation of mankind; protesting with indefatigable energy against all the crimes
of fanaticism and tyranny; pursuing, in all matters of religion,
administration, morals, and law, anything that bore the marks of
tyranny, harshness, or barbarism; invoking the name of nature
to bid kings, captains, magistrates, and priests to show respect
for human life; laying to their charge, with vehemence and
severity, the blood their policy or their indifference still spilled
on the battlefield or on the scaffold; and finally, taking for their
battle cry—*reason, tolerance, humanity.* . . .

Thus, an understanding of the natural rights of man, the belief
that these rights are inalienable and indefeasible, a strongly expressed desire for liberty of thought and letters, of trade and industry, and for the alleviation of the people's suffering, for the
proscription of all penal laws against religious dissenters and the
abolition of torture and barbarous punishments, the desire for a
milder system of criminal legislation and jurisprudence which
should give complete security to the innocent, and for a simpler
civil code, more in conformance with reason and nature, indifference in all matters of religion which now were relegated to the
status of superstitions and political impostures, a hatred of hypocrisy and fanaticism, a contempt for prejudice, zeal for the propagation of enlightenment: all these principles, gradually filtering
down from philosophical works to every class of society whose
education went beyond the catechism and the alphabet, became
the common faith, the badges of all those who were neither
Machiavellians nor fools. In some countries these principles
formed a public opinion sufficiently widespread for even the mass
of the people to show a willingness to be guided by it and to obey
it. For a feeling of humanity, a tender and active compassion for
all the misfortunes that afflict the human race, and a horror of
anything that in the actions of public institutions, or governments, or individuals, adds new pains to those that are natural
and inevitable were the natural consequences of those principles;
and this feeling exhaled from all the writings and all the speeches
of the time, and already its happy influence had been felt in the

laws and the public institutions, even of those nations still subject to despotism. . . .

All errors in politics and morals are based on philosophical errors and these in turn are connected with scientific errors. There is not a religious system nor a supernatural extravagance that is not founded on ignorance of the laws of nature. The inventors, the defenders, of these absurdities could not foresee the successive perfection of the human mind. Convinced that men in their day knew everything that they could ever know and would always believe what they then believed, they confidently supported their idle dreams on the current opinions of their country and their age.

Advances in the physical sciences are all the more fatal to these errors in that they often destroy them without appearing to attack them, and that they can shower on those who defend them so obstinately the humiliating taunt of ignorance.

. . .

The progress of philosophy and the sciences has favored and extended the progress of letters, and this in turn has served to make the study of the sciences easier, and that of philosophy more popular. The sciences and the arts have assisted one another despite the efforts of the ignorant and the foolish to separate them and make them enemies. Scholarship, which seemed doomed by its respect for the past and its deference toward authority always to lend its support to harmful superstitions, has nevertheless contributed to their eradication, for it was able to borrow the torch of a sounder criticism from philosophy and the sciences. It already knew how to weigh up authorities and compare them; it now learned how to bring every authority before the bar of Reason. It had already discounted prodigies, fantastic anecdotes, facts contrary to all probability; but after attacking the evidence on which such absurdities relied; it now learned that all extraordinary facts must always be rejected, however impressive the evidence in their favor, unless this can truly turn the scale against the weight of their physical or moral probability.

Thus all the intellectual activities of man, however different they may be in their aims, their methods, or the qualities of mind they exact, have combined to further the progress of human reason. Indeed, the whole system of human labor is like a well-made machine whose several parts have been systematically distinguished but nonetheless, being intimately bound together, form a single whole and work toward a single end. . . .

But although everything tells us that the human race will never relapse into its former state of barbarism, although everything combines to reassure us against that corrupt and cowardly political theory which would condemn it to oscillate forever between truth and error, liberty and servitude, nevertheless we still see the forces of enlightenment in possession of not more than a very small portion of the globe, and the truly enlightened vastly outnumbered by the great mass of men who are still given over to ignorance and prejudice. We still see vast areas in which men groan in slavery, vast areas offering the spectacle of nations either degraded by the vices of a civilization whose progress is impeded by corruption, or still vegetating in the infant condition of early times. We observe that the labors of recent ages have done much for the progress of the human mind, but little for the perfection of the human race; that they have done much for the honor of man, something for his liberty, but so far, almost nothing for his happiness. At a few points our eyes are dazzled with a brilliant light; but thick darkness still covers an immense stretch of the horizon. There are a few circumstances from which the philosopher can take consolation; but he is still afflicted by the spectacle of the stupidity, slavery, barbarism, and extravagance of mankind; and the friend of humanity can find unmixed pleasure only in tasting the sweet delights of hope for the future. . . .

The Tenth Stage

THE FUTURE PROGRESS OF THE HUMAN MIND

If man can, with almost complete assurance, predict phenomena when he knows their laws, and if, even when he does not, he can still, with great expectation of success, forecast the future on the basis of his experience of the past, why, then, should it be regarded as a fantastic undertaking to sketch, with some pretense to truth, the future destiny of man on the basis of his history? The sole foundation for belief in the natural sciences is this idea, that the general laws directing the phenomena of the universe, known or unknown, are necessary and constant. Why should this principle be any less true for the development of the intellectual and moral faculties of man than for the other operations of nature? Since beliefs founded on past experience of like conditions provide the only rule of conduct for the wisest of men, why should the philosopher be forbidden to base his conjectures on these same foundations, so long as he does not attribute to them a certainty superior to that warranted by the number, the constancy, and the accuracy of his observations?

Our hopes for the future condition of the human race can be subsumed under three important heads: the abolition of inequality between nations, the progress of equality within each nation, and the true perfection of mankind. Will all nations one day attain that state of civilization which the most enlightened, the freest, and the least burdened by prejudices, such as the French and the Anglo-Americans, have attained already? Will the vast gulf that separates these peoples from the slavery of nations under the rule of monarchs, from the barbarism of African tribes, from the ignorance of savages, little by little disappear?

Is there on the face of the earth a nation whose inhabitants have been debarred by nature herself from the enjoyment of freedom and the exercise of reason?

Are those differences which have hitherto been seen in every civilized country in respect of the enlightenment, the resources, and the wealth enjoyed by the different classes into which it is divided, is that inequality between men which was aggravated or perhaps produced by the earliest progress of society, are these part of civilization itself, or are they due to the present imperfections of the social art? Will they necessarily decrease and ultimately make way for a real equality, the final end of the social art, in which even the effects of the natural differences between men will be mitigated and the only kind of inequality to persist will be that which is in the interests of all and which favors the progress of civilization, of education, and of industry, without entailing either poverty, humiliation, or dependence? In other words, will men approach a condition in which everyone will have the knowledge necessary to conduct himself in the ordinary affairs of life, according to the light of his own reason, to preserve his mind free from prejudice, to understand his rights and to exercise them in accordance with his conscience and his creed; in which everyone will become able, through the development of his faculties, to find the means of providing for his needs; and in which at last misery and folly will be the exception, and no longer the habitual lot of a section of society? . . .

Let us turn to the enlightened nations of Europe, and observe the size of their present populations in relation to the size of their territories. Let us consider, in agriculture and industry, the proportion that holds between labor and the means of subsistence, and we shall see that it would be impossible for those means to be kept at their present level and consequently for the population to be kept at its present size if a great number of individuals were not almost entirely dependent for the maintenance of themselves and their family either on their own labor or on the interest from capital invested so as to make their labor more productive. Now both these sources of income depend on the life and even on the health of the head of the family. They provide what is rather like a life annuity, save that it is more dependent on chance; and in consequence there is a very real difference between people living like this and those whose resources are not at all subject to the same risks, who live either on revenue from land, or on the interest on capital which is almost independent of their own labor.

Here, then, is a necessary cause of inequality, or dependence, and even of misery, which ceaselessly threatens the most numerous and most active class in our society.

We shall point out how it can be in great part eradicated by guaranteeing people in old age a means of livelihood produced partly by their own savings and partly by the savings of others who make the same outlay, but who die before they need to reap the reward; or again, on the same principle of compensation, by securing for widows and orphans an income which is the same and costs the same for those families which suffer an early loss and for those which suffer it later; or again, by providing all children with the capital necessary for the full use of their labor, available at the age when they start work and found a family, a capital which increases at the expense of those whom premature death prevents from reaching this age. It is to the application of the calculus to the probabilities of life and the investment of money that we owe the idea of these methods, which have already been successful, although they have not been applied in a sufficiently comprehensive and exhaustive fashion to render them really useful, not merely to a few individuals, but to society as a whole, by making it possible to prevent those periodic disasters which strike at so many families and which are such a recurrent source of misery and suffering.

We shall point out that schemes of this nature, which can be organized in the name of the social authority and become one of its greatest benefits, can also be the work of private associations, which will be formed without any real risk, once the principles for the proper working of these schemes have been widely diffused and the mistakes which have been the undoing of a large number of these associations no longer hold terrors for us. . . .

No one has ever believed that the mind can gain knowledge of all the facts of nature or attain the ultimate means of precision in the measurement, or in the analysis, of the facts of nature, the relations between objects, and all the possible combinations of ideas. Even the relations between magnitudes, the mere notion of quantity or extension, taken in its fullest comprehension, give rise to a system so vast that it will never be mastered by the human mind in its entirety, that there will always be a part of it, always, indeed, the larger part of it, that will remain forever unknown. People have believed that man can never know more than a part of the objects that the nature of his intelligence allows him to understand, and that he must in the end arrive at a point where the number and complexity of the objects that he already knows have absorbed all his strength so that any further progress must be completely impossible.

But since, as the number of known facts increases, the human mind learns how to classify them and to subsume them under more general facts, and at the same time, the instruments and methods employed in their observation and their exact measurement acquire a new precision; since, as more relations between various objects become known, man is able to reduce them to more general relations, to express them more simply, and to present them in such a way that it is possible to grasp a greater number of them with the same degree of intellectual ability and the same amount of application; since, as the mind learns to understand more complicated combinations of ideas, simpler formulas soon reduce their complexity; so truths that were dis-

covered only by great effort, that could at first only be understood
by men capable of profound thought, are soon developed and
proved by methods that are not beyond the reach of common
intelligence. If the methods which have led to these new combinations of ideas are ever exhausted, if their application to
hitherto unsolved questions should demand exertions greater
than either the time or the capacity of the learned would permit, some method of a greater generality or simplicity will be
found so that genius can continue undisturbed on its path. The
strength and the limits of man's intelligence may remain un-
altered; and yet the instruments that he uses will increase and
improve, the language that fixes and determines his ideas will
acquire greater breadth and precision, and, unlike mechanics,
where an increase of force means a decrease of speed, the methods
that lead genius to the discovery of truth increase at once the
force and the speed of its operations. . . .

With all this progress in industry and welfare, which establishes
a happier proportion between men's talents and their needs, each
successive generation will have larger possessions, either as a result
of this progress or through the preservation of the products of
industry; and so, as a consequence of the physical constitution of
the human race, the number of people will increase. Might there
not then come a moment when these necessary laws begin to work
in a contrary direction; when, the number of people in the world
finally exceeding the means of subsistence, there will in consequence ensue a continual diminution of happiness and population, a true retrogression, or at best an oscillation between good
and bad? In societies that have reached this stage will not this
oscillation be a perennial source of more or less periodic disaster?
Will it not show that a point has been attained beyond which all
further improvement is impossible, that the perfectibility of the
human race has after long years arrived at a term beyond which
it may never go?

There is doubtless no one who does not think that such a time
is still very far from us; but will it ever arrive? It is impossible to
pronounce about the likelihood of an event that will occur only
when the human species will have necessarily acquired a degree
of knowledge of which we can have no inkling. And who would
take it upon himself to predict the condition to which the art of

converting the elements to the use of man may in time be brought?

But even if we agree that the limit will one day arrive, nothing follows from it that is in the least alarming as far as either the happiness of the human race or its indefinite perfectibility is concerned; if we consider that, before all this comes to pass, the progress of reason will have kept pace with that of the sciences, and that the absurd prejudices of superstition will have ceased to corrupt and degrade the moral code by its harsh doctrines instead of purifying and elevating it, we can assume that by then men will know that if they have a duty toward those who are not yet born, that duty is not to give them existence but to give them happiness; their aim would be to promote the general welfare of the human race or of the society in which they live or of the family to which they belong, rather than foolishly to encumber the world with useless and wretched beings. It is, then, possible that there should be a limit to the amount of food that can be produced, and consequently, to the size of the population of the world, without this involving that untimely destruction of some of those creatures who have been given life which is so contrary to nature and to social prosperity. . . .

What are we to expect from the perfection of laws and public institutions, consequent upon the progress of those sciences, but the reconciliation, the identification, of the interests of each with the interests of all? Has the social art any other aim save that of destroying their apparent opposition? Will not a country's constitution and laws accord best with the rights of reason and nature when the path of virtue is no longer arduous and when the temptations that lead men from it are few and feeble?

Is there any vicious habit, any practice contrary to good faith, any crime, whose origin and first cause cannot be traced back to the legislation, the institutions, the prejudices, of the country wherein this habit, this practice, this crime, can be observed? In short, will not the general welfare that results from the progress of the useful arts once they are grounded on solid theory, or from the progress of legislation once it is rooted in the truths of political science, incline mankind to humanity, benevolence, and justice? In other words, do not all these observations, which I propose to develop further in my book, show that the moral goodness of man, the necessary consequence of his constitution, is capable of indefinite perfection like all his other faculties, and that nature has linked together in an unbreakable chain truth, happiness, and virtue?

.   .   .

These are the questions with which we shall conclude this final stage. How consoling for the philosopher who laments the errors, the crimes, the injustices, which still pollute the earth and of which he is often the victim in this view of the human race, emancipated from its shackles, released from the empire of fate and from that of the enemies of its progress, advancing with a firm and sure step along the path of truth, virtue, and happiness! It is the contemplation of this prospect that rewards him for all his efforts to assist the progress of reason and the defense of liberty. He dares to regard these strivings as part of the eternal chain of human destiny; and in this persuasion he is filled with the true delight of virtue and the pleasure of having done some lasting good which fate can never destroy by a sinister stroke of revenge, by calling back the reign of slavery and prejudice. Such contemplation is for him an asylum, in which the memory of his persecutors cannot pursue him; there he lives in thought with man restored to his natural rights and dignity, forgets man tormented and corrupted by greed, fear, or envy; there he lives with his peers in an Elysium created by reason and graced by the purest pleasures known to the love of mankind.

PART TWO

The Enlightenment Reconsidered

1   *Cassirer*

Thirty-five major works in philosophy and history by Ernst Cassirer have appeared since 1899, three of them since his death in 1945. The Philosophy of the Enlightenment *was published first in German in 1932, and in English translation in 1951. For all its highly individual quirks of interpretation it remains the standard evaluation of the Enlightenment.*

Taking his cue from Kant, whom he judges the archetypical figure of the age, Cassirer assigns to reason the task of devising a new ethic for the eighteenth century after the dissolution of the old one under the impact of science. But reason as a source and sanction for ethics is carefully defined to show the different ways it was used—Kantian and utilitarian—to secularize the traditional Christian morality. Whether metaphysical or positive, however, whether it is Reason or reasonableness we are talking about, it is the autonomy of the human mind that distinguishes the age from the medieval period that preceded it, and the postmodern one to follow. The Age of Enlightenment, having its roots in the seventeenth century and its fulfillment in the nineteenth, is synonymous with the modern period in history.

SOURCE. Ernst Cassirer, *The Philosophy of the Enlightenment,* translated by Fritz C. A. Koelln and James P. Pettegrove. Copyright 1951 by Princeton University Press: Princeton Paperback, 1968, pp. 5–9, 13–14. Reprinted by permission of Princeton University Press.

THE PHILOSOPHY OF THE ENLIGHTENMENT

"Reason" becomes the unifying and central point of this century, expressing all that it longs and strives for, and all that it achieves. But the historian of the eighteenth century would be guilty of error and hasty judgment if he were satisfied with this characterization and thought it a safe point of departure. For where the century itself sees an end, the historian finds merely a starting-point for his investigation; where the century seems to find an answer, the historian sees his real problem. The eighteenth century is imbued with a belief in the unity and immutability of reason. Reason is the same for all thinking subjects, all nations, all epochs, and all cultures. From the changeability of religious creeds, of moral maxims and convictions, of theoretical opinions and judgments, a firm and lasting element can be extracted which is permanent in itself, and which in this identity and permanence expresses the real essence of reason. For us the word "reason" has long since lost its unequivocal simplicity even if we are in essential agreement with the basic aims of the philosophy of the Enlightenment. We can scarcely use this word any longer without being conscious of its history; and time and again we see how great a change of meaning the term has undergone. This circumstance constantly reminds us how little meaning the terms "reason" and "rationalism" still retain, even in the sense of purely historical characteristics. The general concept is vague, and it becomes clear and distinct only when the right "differentia specifica" is added. Where are we to look for this specific difference in the eighteenth century? If it liked to call itself a "century of reason," a "philosophic century," wherein lies the characteristic and distinguishing features of this designation? In what sense is the word "philosophy" used here? What are its special tasks, and what means are at its disposal for accomplishing these tasks in order to place the doctrines of the world and of man on a firm foundation?

If we compare the answers of the eighteenth century to these questions with the answers prevailing at the time when that century began its intellectual labors, we arrive at a negative distinction. The seventeenth century had seen the real task of philosophy in the construction of the philosophical "system." Truly "philosophical" knowledge had seemed attainable only when thought, starting from a highest being and from a highest, intuitively grasped certainty, succeeded in spreading the light of this certainty over all derived being and all derived knowledge. This was done by the method of proof and rigorous inference, which added other propositions to the first original certainty and in this way pieced out and linked together the whole chain of possible knowledge. No link of this chain could be removed from the whole; none was explicable by itself. The only real explanation possible consisted in its "derivation," in the strict, systematic deduction by which any link might be traced back to the source of being and certainty, by which its distance from this source might be determined, and by which the number of intermediate links separating a given link from this source might be specified. The eighteenth century abandons this kind of deduction and proof. It no longer vies with Descartes and Malebranche, with Leibniz and Spinoza for the prize of systematic rigor and completeness. It seeks another concept of truth and philosophy whose function is to extend the boundaries of both and make them more elastic, concrete, and vital. The Enlightenment does not take the ideal of this mode of thinking from the philosophical doctrines of the past; on the contrary, it constructs its ideal according to the model and pattern of contemporary natural science.

The attempt to solve the central problem of philosophic method involves recourse to Newton's "Rules of Philosophizing" rather than to Descartes' *Discourse on Method,* with the result that philosophy presently takes an entirely new direction. For Newton's method is not that of pure deduction, but that of analysis. He does not begin by setting up certain principles, certain general concepts and axioms, in order, by virtue of abstract inferences, to pave the way to the knowledge of the particular, the "factual." Newton's approach moves in just the opposite direction. His phenomena are the data of experience; his principles are the goal of his investigation. If the latter are first according to nature (πρότερον τῇ φύσει), then the former must always be first to us (πρότερον πρὸς ἡμᾶς). Hence the true method of physics can never consist in proceeding from any arbitrary *a priori* starting-point, from a hypothesis, and in completely developing the logical conclusions implicit in it. For such hypotheses can be invented and modified as desired; logically, any one of them is as valid as any other. We can progress from this logical indifference to the truth and precision of physical science only by applying the measuring stick elsewhere. A scientific abstraction or "definition" cannot serve as a really unambiguous starting-point, for such a starting-point can only be obtained from experience and observation. This does not mean that Newton and his disciples and followers saw a cleavage between experience and thinking, that is, between the realm of bare fact and that of pure thought. No such conflicting modes of validity, no such dualism between "relations of ideas" and "matters of fact" as we find in Hume's *Enquiry concerning Human Understanding,* is to be found among the Newtonian thinkers. For the goal and basic presupposition of Newtonian research is universal order and law in the material world. Such regularity means that facts as such are not mere matter, they are not a jumble of discrete elements; on the contrary, facts exhibit an all-pervasive form. This form appears in mathematical determinations and in arrangements according to measure and number. But such arrangements cannot be foreseen in the mere concept; they must rather be shown to exist in the facts themselves. The procedure is thus not from concepts and axioms to phenomena, but vice versa. Observation produces the datum of science; the principle and law are the object of the investigation.

This new methodological order characterizes all eighteenth century thought. The value of system, the *"esprit systématique,"* is neither underestimated nor neglected; but it is sharply distinguished from the love of system for its own sake, the *"esprit de système."* The whole theory of knowledge of the eighteenth century strives to confirm this distinction. D'Alembert in his "Preliminary Discourse" to the French *Encyclopedia* makes this distinction the central point of his argument, and Condillac in his *Treatise on Systems* gives it explicit form and justification. Condillac tries to subject the great systems of the seventeenth century to the test of historical criticism. He tries to show that each of them failed because, instead of sticking to the facts and developing its concepts from them, it raised some individual concept to the status of a dogma. In opposition to the "spirit of systems" a new alliance is now called for between the "positive" and the "rational" spirit. The positive and the rational are never in conflict, but their true synthesis can only be achieved by the right sort of mediation. One should not seek order, law, and "reason" as a rule that may be grasped and expressed prior to the phenomena, as their *a priori;* one should rather discover such regularity in the phenomena themselves, as the form of their immanent connection. Nor should one attempt to anticipate from the outset such "reason" in the form of a closed system; one should rather permit this reason to unfold gradually, with ever increasing clarity and perfection, as knowledge of the facts progresses. The new logic that is now sought in the conviction that it is everywhere present on the path of knowledge is neither the logic of the scholastic nor of the purely mathematical concept; it is rather the "logic of facts." The mind must abandon itself to the abundance of phenomena and gauge itself constantly by them. For it may be sure that it will not get lost, but that instead it will find here its own real truth and standard. Only in this way can the genuine correlation of subject and object, of truth and reality, be achieved; only so can the correspondence between these concepts, which is the condition of all scientific knowledge, be brought about.

From the actual course of scientific thinking since its revival in modern times the Enlightenment derives its concrete, self-evident proof that this synthesis of the "positive" and the "rational" is not a mere postulate, but that the goal set up is attainable and the ideal fully realizable. In the progress of natural science and the various phases it has gone through, the philosophy of the Enlightenment believes it can, as it were, tangibly grasp its ideal. For here it can follow step by step the triumphal march of the modern analytical spirit. It had been this spirit that in the course of barely a century and a half had conquered all reality, and that now seemed finally to have accomplished its great task of reducing the multiplicity of natural phenomena to a single universal rule.

. . .

We must, of course, abandon all hope of ever wresting from things their ultimate mystery, of ever penetrating to the absolute being of matter or of the human soul. If, however, we refer to empirical law and order, the "inner core of nature" proves by no means inaccessible. In this realm we can establish ourselves and proceed in every direction. The power of reason does not consist in enabling us to transcend the empirical world but rather in teaching us to feel at home in it. Here again is evident a characteristic change of meaning in the concept of reason as compared with seventeenth century usage. In the great metaphysical systems of that century—those of Descartes and Malebranche, of Spinoza and Leibniz—reason is the realm of the "eternal verities," of those truths held in common by the human and the divine mind. What we know through reason, we therefore behold "in God." Every act of reason means participation in the divine nature; it gives access to the intelligible world. The eighteenth century takes reason in a different and more modest sense. It is no longer the sum total of "innate ideas" given prior to all experience, which reveal the absolute essence of things. Reason is now looked upon rather as an acquisition than as a heritage. It is not the treasury of the mind in which the truth like a minted coin lies stored; it is rather the original intellectual force which guides the discovery and determination of truth. This determination is the seed and the indispensable presupposition of all real certainty. The whole eighteenth century understands reason in this sense; not as a sound body of knowledge, principles, and truths, but as a kind of energy, a force which is fully comprehensible only in its agency and effects. What reason is, and what it can do, can never be known by its results but only by its function. And its most important function consists in its power to bind and to dissolve. It dissolves everything merely factual, all simple data of experience, and everything believed on the evidence of revelation, tradition and authority; and it does not rest content until it has analyzed all these things into their simplest component parts and into their last elements of belief and opinion. Following this work of dissolution begins the work of construction. Reason cannot stop with the dispersed parts; it has to build from them a new structure, a true whole. But since reason creates this whole and fits the parts together according to its own rule, it gains complete knowledge of the structure of its product. Reason understands this structure because it can reproduce it in its totality and in the ordered sequence of its individual elements. Only in this twofold intellectual movement can the concept of reason be fully characterized, namely, as a concept of agency, not of being.

A.   MEDIEVAL OR MODERN

1   *Becker*

Carl Lotus Becker was an illustrious American historian who took the Enlightenment, on both sides of the Atlantic, as his province. The Heavenly City of the Eighteenth-Century Philosophers *(delivered as a series of lectures in 1931 and published in 1932) has profoundly influenced two generations of historians. In it Becker states that the eighteenth-century philosophers were less modern than they knew. With wit and insight, he argues that they dismantled the heavenly city of Saint Augustine, only to rebuild it with new materials. For all their secularism they were inspired by a faith in certain values that were essentially religious—a faith we no longer possess. There was less of a difference, he says, between the thirteenth and eighteenth centuries than there is between the eighteenth and our own, which seems in many ways to have departed altogether from the main current of Western civilization. The case Becker makes is flawed, and we can argue for or against it, but it seems that we cannot argue without it.*

SOURCE. Carl Becker, *The Heavenly City of the Eighteenth-Century Philosophers* (New Haven, 1932). Copyright © 1932 by Yale University Press.

THE HEAVENLY CITY OF THE
EIGHTEENTH-CENTURY PHILOSOPHERS

Professor Whitehead has recently restored to circulation a seventeenth-century phrase—"climate of opinion." The phrase is much needed. Whether arguments command assent or not depends less upon the logic that conveys them than upon the climate of opinion in which they are sustained. What renders Dante's argument or St. Thomas' definition meaningless to us is not bad logic or want of intelligence, but the medieval climate of opinion—those instinctively held preconceptions in the broad sense, that *Weltanschauung* or world pattern—which imposed upon Dante and St. Thomas a peculiar use of the intelligence and a special type of logic. To understand why we cannot easily follow Dante or St. Thomas it is necessary to understand (as well as may be) the nature of this climate of opinion.

It is well known that the medieval world pattern, deriving from Greek logic and the Christian story, was fashioned by the church which for centuries imposed its authority upon the isolated and anarchic society of western Europe. The modern mind, which curiously notes and carefully describes everything, can indeed describe this climate of opinion although it cannot live in it. In this climate of opinion it was an unquestioned fact that the world and man in it had been created in six days by God the Father, an omniscient and benevolent intelligence, for an ultimate if inscrutable purpose. Although created perfect, man had through disobedience fallen from grace into sin and error, thereby incurring the penalty of eternal damnation. Yet happily a way of atonement and salvation had been provided through the propitiatory sacrifice of God's only begotten son. Helpless in themselves to avert the just wrath of God, men were yet to be permitted, through his mercy, and by humility and obedience to his will, to obtain pardon for sin and error. Life on earth was but a means to this desired end, a temporary probation for the testing of God's children. In God's appointed time, the Earthly City would come to an end, the earth itself be swallowed up in flames. On that last day good and evil men would be finally separated. For the recalcitrant there was reserved a place of everlasting punishment; but the faithful would be gathered with God in the Heavenly City, there in perfection and felicity to dwell forever.

Existence was thus regarded by the medieval man as a cosmic drama, composed by the master dramatist according to a central theme and on a rational plan. Finished in idea before it was enacted in fact, before the world began written down to the last syllable of recorded time, the drama was unalterable either for good or evil. There it was, precisely defined, to be understood as far as might be, but at all events to be remorselessly played out to its appointed end. The duty of man was to accept the drama as written, since he could not alter it; his function, to play the rôle assigned. That he might play his rôle according to the divine text, subordinate authorities—church and state—deriving their just powers from the will of God, were instituted among men to dispose them to submission and to instruct them in their proper lines. Intelligence was essential, since God had endowed men with it. But the function of intelligence was strictly limited. Useless to inquire curiously into the origin or final state of existence, since both had been divinely determined and sufficiently revealed. Useless, even impious, to inquire into its ultimate meaning, since God alone could fully understand it. The function of intelligence was therefore to demonstrate the truth of revealed knowledge, to reconcile diverse and pragmatic experience with the rational pattern of the world as given in faith.

Under the bracing influence of this climate of opinion the best thought of the time assumed a thoroughly rationalistic form. I know it is the custom to call the thirteenth century an age of faith, and to contrast it with the eighteenth century, which is thought to be preëminently the age of reason. In a sense the distinction is true enough, for the word "reason," like other words, has many meanings. Since eighteenth-century writers employed reason to discredit Christian dogma, a "rationalist" in common parlance came to mean an "unbeliever," one who denied the truth of Christianity. In this sense Voltaire was a rationalist, St. Thomas a man of faith. But this use of the word is unfortunate, since it obscures the fact that reason may be employed to support faith as well as to destroy it. There were, certainly, many differences between Voltaire and St. Thomas, but the two men had much in common for all that. What they had in common was the profound conviction that their beliefs could be reasonably demonstrated. In a very real sense it may be said of the eighteenth century that it was an age of faith as well as of reason, and of the thirteenth century that it was an age of reason as well as of faith.

. . .

What then can we—scientists, historians, philosophers of the twentieth century—make of the theology-history, the philosophy-science, the dialectic-methodology of the thirteenth century? We can—must, indeed, since that is our habit—peruse with infinite attention and indifference the serried, weighty folios of the *Summa* and such works now carefully preserved in libraries. We can perhaps wonder a little—although, since nothing is alien to us, we are rarely caught wondering—at the unfailing zest, the infinite patience, the extraordinary ingenuity and acumen therein displayed. We can even understand what is therein recorded well enough to translate it clumsily into modern terms. The one thing we cannot do with the *Summa* of St. Thomas is to meet its arguments on their own ground. We can neither assent to them nor refute them. It does not even occur to us to make the effort, since we instinctively feel that in the climate of opinion which sustains such arguments we could only gasp for breath. Its conclusions seem to us neither true nor false, but only irrelevant; and they seem irrelevant because the world pattern into which they are so dexterously woven is no longer capable of eliciting from us either an emotional or an aesthetic response.

With the best will in the world it is quite impossible for us to conceive of existence as a divinely ordered drama, the beginning and end of which is known, the significance of which has once for all been revealed. For good or ill we must regard the world as a continuous flux, a ceaseless and infinitely complicated process of waste and repair, so that "all things and principles of things" are to be regarded as no more than "inconstant modes or fashions," as the "concurrence, renewed from moment to moment, of forces parting sooner or later on their way." The beginning of this continuous process of change is shrouded in impenetrable mist; the end seems more certain, but even less engaging.

. . .

Edit and interpret the conclusions of modern science as ten-

derly as we like, it is still quite impossible for us to regard man
as the child of God for whom the earth was created as a temporary habitation. Rather must be regard him as little more than
a chance deposit on the surface of the world, carelessly thrown
up between two ice ages by the same forces that rust iron and
ripen corn, a sentient organism endowed by some happy or unhappy accident with intelligence indeed, but with an intelligence
that is conditioned by the very forces that it seeks to understand
and to control. The ultimate cause of this cosmic process of
which man is a part, whether God or electricity or a "stress in
the ether," we know not. Whatever it may be, if indeed it be
anything more than a necessary postulate of thought, it appears
in its effects as neither benevolent nor malevolent, as neither
kind nor unkind, but merely as indifferent to us. What is man
that the electron should be mindful of him! Man is but a
foundling in the cosmos, abandoned by the forces that created
him. Unparented, unassisted and undirected by omniscient or
benevolent authority, he must fend for himself, and with the aid
of his own limited intelligence find his way about in an indifferent universe.

Such is the world pattern that determines the character and
direction of modern thinking. The pattern has been a long time
in the weaving. It has taken eight centuries to replace the conception of existence as divinely composed and purposeful drama
by the conception of existence as a blindly running flux of dis-
integrating energy. But there are signs that the substitution is
now fully accomplished; and if we wished to reduce eight centuries of intellectual history to an epigram, we could not do
better than to borrow the words of Aristophanes, "Whirl is king,
having deposed Zeus."

. . .

What can we do? Reason and logic cry out in pain no doubt;
but we have long since learned not to bother overmuch with
reason and logic. Logic was formerly visualized as something
outside us, something existing independently which, if we were
willing, could take us by the hand and lead us into the paths of
truth. We now suspect that it is something the mind has created
to conceal its timidity and keep up its courage, a hocus-pocus
designed to give formal validity to conclusions we are willing to
accept if everybody else in our set will too. If all men are mortal

(an assumption), and if Socrates was a man (in the sense assumed), no doubt Socrates must have been mortal; but we suspect that we somehow knew all this before it was submitted to the test of a syllogism. Logics have a way of multiplying in response to the changes in point of view. First there was one logic, then there were two, then there were several; so that now, according to one authority (if a contributor to the *Encyclopaedia Britannica* who ventures to employ humor can be an authority), the state of logic is "that of Israel under the Judges, every man doeth that which is right in his own eyes." With all due allowance made for mathematical logic (which has to do with concepts, not with facts), and for the logic of probability (which Mr. Keynes assures us has a probable validity), the secure foundations of deductive and inductive logic have been battered to pieces by the ascertainable facts, so that we really have no choice; we must cling to the ascertainable facts though they slay us.

Physicists, therefore, stick to the ascertainable facts. If logic presumes to protest in the name of the law, they know how to square it, so that it complaisantly looks the other way while they go on with illicit enterprises—with the business, for example (it is Sir William Bragg who vouches for it), of teaching "the wave theory of light on Monday, Wednesday, and Friday, and the quantum theory on Tuesday, Thursday, and Saturday."

. . .

Perhaps I have said enough to suggest that the essential quality of the modern climate of opinion is factual rather than rational. The atmosphere which sustains our thought is so saturated with the actual that we can easily do with a minimum of the theoretical. We necessarily look at our world from the point of view of history and from the point of view of science. Viewed historically, it appears to be something in the making, something which can at best be only tentatively understood since it is not yet finished. Viewed scientifically, it appears as something to be accepted, something to be manipulated and mastered, something to adjust ourselves to with the least possible stress. So long as we can make efficient use of things, we feel no irresistible need to understand them. No doubt it is for this reason chiefly that the modern mind can be so wonderfully at ease in a mysterious universe.

. . .

We are accustomed to think of the eighteenth century as es-

sentially modern in its temper. Certainly, the *Philosophes* themselves made a great point of having renounced the superstition
and hocus-pocus of medieval Christian thought, and we have
usually been willing to take them at their word. Surely, we say,
the eighteenth century was preëminently the age of reason,
surely the *Philosophes* were a skeptical lot, atheists in effect if
not by profession, addicted to science and the scientific method,
always out to crush the infamous, valiant defenders of liberty,
equality, fraternity, freedom of speech, and what you will. All
very true. And yet I think the *Philosophes* were nearer the
Middle Ages, less emancipated from the preconceptions of medieval Christian thought, than they quite realized or we have commonly supposed. If we have done them more (or is it less?) than
justice in giving them a good modern character, the reason is
that they speak a familiar language. We read Voltaire more
readily than Dante, and follow an argument by Hume more
easily than one by Thomas Aquinas. But I think our appreciation is of the surface more than of the fundamentals of their
thought. We agree with them more readily when they are witty
and cynical than when they are wholly serious. Their negations
rather than their affirmations enable us to treat them as kindred
spirits.

But, if we examine the foundations of their faith, we find that
at every turn the *Philosophes* betray their debt to medieval
thought without being aware of it. They denounced Christian
philosophy, but rather too much, after the manner of those who
are but half emancipated from the "superstitions" they scorn.
They had put off the fear of God, but maintained a respectful
attitude toward the Deity. They ridiculed the idea that the
universe had been created in six days, but still believed it to be a
beautifully articulated machine designed by the Supreme Being
according to a rational plan as an abiding place for mankind.
The Garden of Eden was for them a myth, no doubt, but they
looked enviously back to the golden age of Roman virtue, or
across the waters to the unspoiled innocence of an Arcadian
civilization that flourished in Pennsylvania. They renounced the
authority of church and Bible, but exhibited a naïve faith in the
authority of nature and reason. They scorned metaphysics, but
were proud to be called philosophers. They dismantled heaven,
somewhat prematurely it seems, since they retained their faith

in the immortality of the soul. They courageously discussed atheism, but not before the servants. They defended toleration valiantly, but could with difficulty tolerate priests. They denied that miracles ever happened, but believed in the perfectibility of the human race. We feel that these Philosophers were at once too credulous and too skeptical. They were the victims of common sense. In spite of their rationalism and their humane sympathies, in spite of their aversion to hocus-pocus and enthusiasm and dim perspectives, in spite of their eager skepticism, their engaging cynicism, their brave youthful blasphemies and talk of hanging the last king in the entrails of the last priest—in spite of all of it, there is more of Christian philosophy in the writings of the *Philosophes* than has yet been dreamt of in our histories.

In the following lectures I shall endeavor to elaborate this theme. I shall attempt to show that the underlying preconceptions of eighteenth-century thought were still, allowance made for certain important alterations in the bias, essentially the same as those of the thirteenth century. I shall attempt to show that the *Philosophes* demolished the Heavenly City of St. Augustine only to rebuild it with more up-to-date materials.

. . .

Alas yes, that is, indeed, the fact! The eighteenth-century Philosophers, like the medieval scholastics, held fast to a revealed body of knowledge, and they were unwilling or unable to learn anything from history which could not, by some ingenious trick played on the dead, be reconciled with their faith. Their faith, like the faith by which any age lives, was born of their experience and their needs; and since their experience and their needs were in deadly conflict with the traditional and established and still powerful philosophy of church and state, the articles of their faith were at every point opposed to those of the established philosophy. The essential articles of the religion of the Enlightenment may be stated thus: (1) man is not natively depraved; (2) the end of life is life itself, the good life on earth instead of the beatific life after death; (3) man is capable, guided solely by the light of reason and experience, of perfecting the good life on earth; and (4) the first and essential condition of the good life on earth is the freeing of men's minds from the bonds of ignorance and superstition, and of their bodies from the arbitrary oppression of the constituted social authorities. With this creed the "constant and universal principles of human nature," which Hume tells us are to be discovered by a study of history, must be in accord, and "man in general" must be a creature who would conveniently illustrate these principles. What these "universal principles" were the Philosophers, therefore, understood before they went in search of them, and with "man in general" they were well acquainted, having created him in their own image. They knew instinctively that "man in general" is natively good, easily enlightened, disposed to follow reason and common sense; generous and humane and tolerant, more easily led by persuasion than compelled by force; above all a good citizen and a man of virtue, being well aware that, since the rights claimed by himself are only the natural and imprescriptible rights of all men, it is necessary for him voluntarily to assume the obligations and to submit to the restraints imposed by a just government for the commonweal.

.   .   .

I have already stated, more than once perhaps, that the Philosophers were not professional philosophers sitting in cool ivory towers for contemplative purposes only, but crusaders whose mission it was to recover the holy places of the religion of humanity from Christian philosophy and the infamous things that supported it. The directing impulse of their thought was that mankind had been corrupted and betrayed by false doctrines. Their essential task was to destroy these false doctrines; and in order to do so they had of course to meet the doctrines of Christian philosophy with opposed doctrines, contrary ideas. But not with radically different ideas, not with ideas of a different order altogether, since it is true of ideas, as of men, that they cannot fight unless they occupy the same ground: ideas that rush toward each other on different levels of apprehension will pass without conflict or mutual injury because they never establish contact, never collide. In order to defeat Christian philosophy the Philosophers had therefore to meet it on the level of certain common preconceptions. They could never rout the enemy by denying that human life is a significant drama— the notion was too widely, too unconsciously held, even by the Philosophers themselves, for that; but, admitting that human life is significant drama, the Philosophers could claim that the Christian version of the drama was a false and pernicious one; and their best hope of displacing the Christian version lay in recasting it, and in bringing it up to date. In short, the task of the Philosophers was to present another interpretation of the past, the present, and the future state of mankind.

. . .

The eighteenth-century Philosophers might therefore rewrite the story of man's first state, relegating the Garden of Eden to the limbo of myths; they might discover a new revelation in the book of nature to displace the revelation in Holy Writ; they might demonstrate that reason, supported by the universal assent of mankind as recorded in history, was a more infallible authority than church and state—they might well do all this and yet find their task but half finished. No "return," no "rebirth" of classical philosophy, however idealized and humanized, no worship of ancestors long since dead, or pale imitations of Greek pessimism would suffice for a society that had been so long and so well taught to look forward to another and better world to come. Without a new heaven to replace the old, a new way of salvation, of attaining perfection, the religion of humanity would appeal in vain to the common run of men.

The new heaven had to be located somewhere within the confines of the earthly life, since it was an article of philosophical faith that the end of life is life itself, the perfected temporal life of man; and in the future, since the temporal life was not yet perfected. But if the celestial heaven was to be dismantled in order to be rebuilt on earth, it seemed that the salvation of mankind must be attained, not by some outside, miraculous, catastrophic agency (God or the philosopher-king), but by man himself, by the progressive improvement made by the efforts of successive generations of men; and in this coöperative enterprise posterity had its undeniable uses: posterity would complete what the past and the present had begun. "We have admired our ancestors less," said Chastellux, "but we have loved our contemporaries better, and have expected more of our descendants." Thus, the Philosophers called in posterity to exorcise the double illusion of the Christian paradise and the golden age of antiquity. For the love of God they substituted love of humanity; for the vicarious atonement the perfectibility of man through his own efforts; and for the hope of immortality in another world the hope of living in the memory of future generations.

. . .

It was more especially in France, where social discontent was most acute, that the doctrine of progress, of perfectibility, became an essential article of faith in the new religion of humanity. Fontenelle had thought of progress in terms of the gradual increase in knowledge and correct reasoning. It did not occur to him, or to many of his contemporaries, to look forward to any radical regeneration of morals or of social institutions. To play with the idea of utopia, as described by Plato or Thomas More or Bacon, was an engaging pastime no doubt; to project it, as something to be practically realized, into the future history of France, would have seemed to him scarcely less an illusion than the naïve dream of perfection in the Garden of Eden. Yet this is just what, under the pressure of social discontents, came to pass: the utopian dream of perfection, that necessary compensation for the limitations and frustrations of the present state, having been long identified with the golden age or the Garden of Eden or life eternal in the Heavenly City of God, and then by the sophisticated transferred to remote or imagined lands (the moon or Atlantis or Nowhere, Tahiti or Pennsylvania or Peking), was at last projected into the life of man on earth and identified with the desired and hoped-for regeneration of society.

This transformation of the old utopian dream may be followed in the writings of the Philosophers: not alone in those well-known formal treatises on the subject of progress—Turgot's discourses, Lessing's *Education of the Human Race,* Herder's *Ideas on the Philosophy of the History of Mankind,* Condorcet's *Sketch of the Progress of the Human Spirit;* but equally well in the writings of other Philosophers, in writings not immediately concerned with that subject. The Philosophers were, almost without exception, much concerned with progress, perfectibility, the fate of posterity; and this interest, needless to say, was intimately associated with their interest in history. The past, the present, and the future state of mankind were for them but aspects of the same preoccupation. The Philosophers were, after all, primarily concerned with the present state of things, which they wished to change; and they needed good reasons for their desire to change it. They wished to justify their discontents, to validate their aversions; and they accomplished this object by enlarging the social specious present, by projecting the present state into the centuries, where it could be seen to be but a passing unhappy phase of the universal experience of mankind.

In this enterprise posterity played an important rôle: it replaced God as judge and justifier of those virtuous and enlightened ones who were not of this world. All men in some degree need outside approval for what they think and do—the approval of loved ones, of kith and kin, of the community of right-minded men. Most men in all times obtain the required approval by following the established customs and professing the common opinions. But there are always some eccentric individuals, and on occasion certain groups, who find the present temporal world of men and things intolerable. So they withdraw from it, living in spiritual exile, or else they endeavor to transform it. In either case they are likely to lose the approval of the community, and losing the approval of the community they seek the approval of some power above or beyond it, of some authority more universally valid than that of the present world of men and things: they seek the approval of God, or the law of nature, or the inevitable class conflict, or the force outside themselves that makes for righteousness. The isolated ones, like Archimedes, find that without a fulcrum upon which to rest their lever they cannot move the inert and resistant world of men and things as they are. The eighteenth-century revolutionists, whether in thought or in deed, responded to this need. Finding themselves out of harmony with the temporary world of men and things, they endeavored to put themselves in tune with the infinite powers: over against the ephemeral customs and mores, they set the universal laws of nature and of nature's God; from the immediate judgments of men, they appealed to the universal judgment of humanity. Humanity was an abstraction, no doubt; but through the beneficent law of progress the wisdom of the ages would be accumulated, transmitted, and placed at the disposal of posterity. Every age would be the posterity of all preceding ages; and as the eighteenth century, in the light of two thousand years of human experience, had vindicated Socrates and Regulus against the erring opinion of their times, so generations yet to come would vindicate the Voltaires and the Rousseaus, the Robespierres and the Rolands.

I do not know why historians, who are ardently devoted to noting exactly what happened, should so generally have failed to note a fact that is writ large in the most authentic documents: the fact that the thought of posterity was apt to elicit from eighteenth-century Philosophers and revolutionary leaders a highly emotional, an essentially religious, response. Posterity, like nature, was often personified, reverently addressed as a divinity, and invoked in the accents of prayer. This, too, is a fact to be recorded, as curious and interesting as many another on which historians have lavished their erudition. I take at random an example of this phenomenon. Robespierre is speaking before the Jacobin Club on the question of war with Austria, and he ends his speech with the following invocation:

O posterity, sweet and tender hope of humanity, thou art not a stranger to us; it is for thee that we brave all the blows of tyranny; it is thy happiness which is the price of our painful struggles: often discouraged by the obstacles that surround us, we feel the need of thy consolations; it is to thee that we confide the task of completing our labors, and the destiny of all the unborn generations of men! . . . May the martyrs of liberty occupy in thy memory the place which the heroes of imposture and aristocracy have usurped in ours; . . . may thy first impulse be to scorn traitors and hate tyrants; may thy motto be: protection, love, benevolence to the unhappy, eternal war to oppressors! Make haste, O posterity, to bring to pass the hour of equality, of justice, of happiness![1]

. . .

2   *Gay*

In 1956 Peter Gay, now professor of history at Yale University, participated in a symposium to assess the significance of Carl Becker's Heavenly City of the Eighteenth-Century Philosophers. *The paper he read there appeared first in the* Political Science Quarterly, *June, 1957, under the title, "Carl Becker's Heavenly City," and was reprinted in a volume called,* Carl Becker's Heavenly City Revisited, *published by the Cornell University*

---

[1] C. Vellay, *Discours et rapports de Robespierre* (1908), p. 155. Cf. *Journal des débats de la société des amis de la constitution* (January, 1792), No. 127, p. 3.

SOURCE. Peter Gay, "Carl Becker's Heavenly City," in Raymond O. Rockwood: *Carl Becker's Heavenly City Revisited.* © 1958 by Cornell University. Used by permission of Cornell University Press.

Press in 1958. Gay's article describes the problem of persistence and change in history, and argues quite rightly that the Enlightenment produced a new civilization out of the remnants of the medieval one. If those changes that transpired between the thirteenth and eighteenth centuries were relatively unimportant ones, as Becker would have it, then how do we go about judging significant change in history? Philosophers might argue that there is nothing new under the sun, but the historian, by the nature of his craft, has to deal with the fact of change. The eighteenth century philosophers were correct in noting the progress made since the Middle Ages, and by that token we might note that modern history and historiography began with the fact and idea of progress in the Age of Enlightenment.

CARL BECKER'S HEAVENLY CITY

"Before estimating a book it is well to read its title with care," Becker suggests, and the title of this book briefly states its central theme: the *philosophes* destroyed less well than they knew.[1] They were believers in their most skeptical moods, Christians in their most anti-Christian diatribes:

"In spite of their rationalism and their humane sympathies, in spite of their aversion to hocus-pocus and enthusiasm and dim perspectives, in spite of their eager skepticism, their engaging cynicism, their brave youthful blasphemies and talk of hanging the last king in the entrails of the last priest—in spite of all of it, there is more of Christian philosophy in the writings of the *Philosophes* than has yet been dreamt of in our histories. . . . I shall attempt to show that the *Philosophes* demolished the Heavenly City of St. Augustine only to rebuild it with more up-to-date materials."[2]

Before launching upon this theme, Becker expounds a general assumption about the relation of change to permanence in

---

[1] For Becker's remark, see *The Heavenly City*, 115. It has been said (and Becker himself said it jokingly) that *The Heavenly City* is not history at all but a moral tract. If it is not history at all, it should certainly not be recommended as good history.

[2] *Ibid.*, 31.

history. There is change in history: Thomas Aquinas and David Hume both used the word "reason" but meant very different things by it, so that to compare their philosophies by investigating simply what they said about "reason" would do injustice to both. Words persist, but their meanings change. But also there is permanence in history: no era wholly liberates itself from its antecedents, although its spokesmen may proudly (or perhaps anxiously) proclaim that they have made a complete break. Rhetoric may change while ideas persist. Becker suggests that intellectual historians must reckon with this dialectic of permanence and change and must be misled neither by spurious novelty nor by spurious persistence.[3]

This historiographical warning is the most valuable idea in *The Heavenly City;* unfortunately, Becker fails to heed it when he elaborates his thesis. He argues that despite the great change in the climate of opinion between the thirteenth and eighteenth centuries the two centuries were far more closely related than would immediately appear or would be admitted by the *philosophes.* The *philosophes'* claim to be modern must therefore be discounted:

"I know it is the custom to call the thirteenth century an age of faith, and to contrast it with the eighteenth century, which is thought to be preëminently an age of reason. . . . In a very real sense it may be said of the eighteenth century that it was an age of faith as well as of reason, and of the thirteenth century that it was an age of reason as well as of faith."[4]

[3] I hope to expand my remarks on what I have here called "spurious persistence" in a forthcoming article dealing with periodization.

[4] *Heavenly City,* 8. Becker's use of the term "Climates of Opinion" as the heading to his first chapter suggests, correctly, that he relied heavily on Whitehead's *Science and the Modern World* (New York, 1925). Becker repeatedly quotes or paraphrases Whitehead's book without indicating his source—a sign not of unwillingness to give credit, of course, but of Becker's conviction that Whitehead's views are generally known and accepted. Whitehead describes the eighteenth century as the "age of reason, based upon faith" and asserts that "*les philosophes* were not philosophers." They were men who hated "dim perspectives." Whitehead, like Becker, appreciated the *philosophes:* he admired their humaneness, their hatred of cant and cruelty. But like Becker he did not think they were quite first-rate: "If men cannot live on bread alone," he remarks with reference to Voltaire, "still less can they do so on disinfectants." All these formulations reappear in *The Heavenly City.*

The overriding fault of the *philosophes* was their naïveté: they "exhibited a naïve faith in the authority of nature and reason."[5]

This is to fall into the trap of what I have called spurious persistence. It is true that the medieval Catholic rationalists, of whom Thomas Aquinas was the most prominent, assigned to reason an important place in their epistemologies. It is also true —and Becker's reminders are valuable—that the *philosophes* depended upon some unexamined premises which, to the extent that they were unexamined, may be called "faith."

But Becker infers far too much from this. Aquinas' rationalism was by no means as characteristic of the thirteenth century as Voltaire's empiricism was of the eighteenth century. Moreover, Becker forgets his own caution that words may be used in many different ways when he argues that "there were, certainly, many differences between Voltaire and St. Thomas, but the two men had much in common for all that. What they had in common was the profound conviction that their beliefs could be reasonably demonstrated."[6] But the point is precisely that the two philosophers differed over what constitutes reasonable demonstration. For Aquinas reasonable demonstration was deductive and definitional;[7] Voltaire derided such demonstrations as "metaphysics," as examples of the despised *esprit de système*.

.   .   .

Becker plays the same verbal game in his assertion that both centuries were centuries of faith. The word "faith" usually serves to describe two rather different psychological processes. Thirteenth-century faith (if I may simplify a complex matter) was submission, not necessarily to what was absurd, but to what was beyond proof and, after a certain point, beyond argument. Failure to have faith (as Voltaire put it facetiously) led to burning in this world and in the next. Eighteenth-century faith in reason, while perhaps often naïve, should be designated by the more neutral term "confidence." Its affirmations were public, open to examination and refutation. "Faith in reason" meant simply that

5 *Heavenly City,* 30. Becker does say that "Voltaire was an optimist, although not a naïve one" (*ibid.,* 37).

6 *Ibid.,* 8.

7 Becker himself quotes a characteristic specimen of Aquinas' deductive method of arguing (*ibid.,* 3). Here as in many other places in the book Becker provides material for the refutation of his case.

for the *philosophes* the method of reason (strictly speaking the scientific method of such natural philosophers as Newton) was superior to other methods of gaining knowledge; it was superior to revelation, authority, tradition, because it was more reliable.[8] In Diderot's pornographic novel, *Les bijoux indiscrets,* there is a charming dream: the dreamer sees himself transported into a building that has no foundations and whose columns rise into the mists. The crowds walking in and around the building are crippled and deformed old men. It is the land of hypothesis, and the cripples are the makers of systems. But there is a vigorous small child, growing into a giant as the dream progresses, who draws near the fantastic building and destroys it with one blow. That giant is Experiment—no dweller of the heavenly city. Did not the *philosophes,* in their reveries, see themselves as that giant? And did they not include thinkers like Aquinas among the lame makers of systems? To denounce the *philosophes* for having faith in reason may be witty, but the paradox solves no problems in intellectual history.

. . .

Becker's generalizations are indefensible not because they are too general—most generalizations are—but because some of them are inadequately explored, some are misleading, and others are simply wrong.

. . .

"They ridiculed the idea that the universe had been created in six days, but still believed it to be a beautifully articulated machine designed by the Supreme Being according to a rational plan as an abiding place for mankind." True, but why "but"? There is nothing essentially Christian about this idea of "cosmos" —it had been the foundation of Stoic philosophy. There is nothing essentially Christian about this idea of God as architect —the watchmaker argument for the existence of God, a favorite with the *philosophes,* appears prominently in the discourses of

---

8 I do not wish to assert that the *philosophes* were always consistent or thorough-going empiricists. Rousseau, who showed his respect for empirical knowledge in books III and IV of the *Contrat social* and in the other late political works, could write in the *Discours sur l'inégalité,* "Let us begin by laying facts aside, since they do not affect the question." But he was seeking to elucidate the foundations of morality, and if he did not ask a factual question he was not, after all, seeking a factual answer.

Epictetus. The beautifully articulated machine of the *philosophes* is not a Christian but a pagan machine. What is remarkable is not the supposed resemblance of this machine to Christianity but its always implicit and often explicit repudiation of miracles: God acts through general and uniform laws alone. Here as elsewhere Becker exploits parallels or similarities or correspondences between Christian and *philosophe* thought to claim that the two are identical or that, at the least, the latter is the direct descendant of the former. This has as much logical merit as the assertion that, since Calvin was a determinist and d'Holbach was a determinist, d'Holbach was a Calvinist.

. . .

"They scorned metaphysics, but were proud to be called philosophers." True again, but it is hard to see what this sentence proves. A philosopher is a man who loves knowledge, and when he rejects authority, revelation, system making, he may argue that in his empiricism he is the only *true* philosopher, while his forerunners were idle dreamers. This may be a justified or an unjustified claim, but it does not make the *philosophes* Christians.

. . .

What then has become of Becker's thesis that the *philosophes* did not know what they were doing and were rebuilding the old heavenly city, only with new materials? Without wishing to be paradoxical for the sake of paradox, let me suggest that Becker's formulation turns the truth upside down: the *philosophes* knew exactly what they were doing; they were building a new, earthly city. And in building it they used, along with much new material, some of the old Christian bricks. Far from being less modern than they knew, they were even more modern than they claimed.

. . .

But it is not mistakes such as these that really disappoint the reader in this charming book; the disappointment is, I think, more profound. *The Heavenly City,* as I have said, begins with a significant truth: history is concerned with the dialectical struggle between persistence and change. The eighteenth century is a century in which this struggle becomes peculiarly dramatic and complex, and the opportunities for fruitful research are great. Becker rightly urges the reader to ask searching questions, but he continually suggests the wrong answers. He argues for persistence where there was change, and he argues for one kind of persistence when there was really another.

The *philosophes* lived in an epoch in which the vitality of Christianity was waning and in which natural science, the centralized state, the development of industrial capitalism, imposed the need for a new world view. In building their earthly city, the *philosophes* fashioned their materials from the most varied sources: Christianity, a revived Stoicism and Epicureanism, and a pragmatic recognition of the needs of the new state and the new economy. In their battle for liberation from the old standards and in their search for new standards they experienced the difficulties that any individual struggling for autonomy must face. They contradicted themselves; they failed to see all the implications of their ideas; they sometimes used old words to describe new things; they sometimes used rhetoric that was inappropriate to their ideas. All these questions *The Heavenly City* resolves—wrongly, I believe—with the too simple formula of its title.

The failure of the book is all the more paradoxical in view of Becker's own position. His criticisms of the *philosophes* were from the inside; as Leo Gershoy has said, Carl Becker "had always remained a believer at heart. . . . He had rejoined Voltaire and Condorcet and Wells and all the goodly company who wished humanity well."[9] But in his impatience with his intellectual forebears—an impatience which is always so much greater with those whom you admire than with those you detest—he portrayed the *philosophes* as naïve and as a little fraudulent. Becker was no conservative, but the conservative implications of *The Heavenly City* are plain.

And *The Heavenly City* failed in another, and even more paradoxical, way—through its success. Carl Becker dedicated *Everyman His Own Historian* to those who had assisted him in clarifying his ideas, "chiefly by avoiding the error of Hway, a pupil of Confucius. Hway, said Confucius, is of no assistance to me; there is nothing that I say in which he does not delight." In the twenty-five years that the book has been before the public, the error of Hway has not been avoided. It is time we admitted that Carl Becker's critique of the *philosophes,* like Samuel Johnson's critique of Shakespeare, had every virtue save one, the virtue of being right.

9 Introduction, in Carl Becker, *Progress and Power* (New York, 1949), p. xxxvii.

B. GOOD OR BAD

1   *Crocker*

*Lester G. Crocker, Dean of Humanities at Case Western Reserve
University, has written numerous books and articles on the Enlightenment. In two large and significant volumes,* An Age of
Crisis: Man and World in Eighteenth-Century French Thought,
and Nature and Culture: Ethical Thought in the French Enlightenment, *he argues that what is worst in the contemporary world
has its roots in the secular relativism of eighteenth century
thought; that with the break-down in the medieval synthesis to
which the* philosophes *contributed by their attack on religion, no
new synthesis was created that would hold together. Ultimately
political power came to decide all ethical questions. This is not to
say that the* philosophes *intended it so, but that their ideas did
have consequences that are all too familiar to us. They must share
the responsibility, therefore, for the debacle the twentieth century
has experienced.*

*There are serious criticisms to be leveled against this argument,
which is not a new one, but the thesis is ably presented by Crocker
in the book excerpted here,* An Age of Crisis: Man and World in
Eighteenth-Century French Thought (Baltimore, Johns Hopkins
Press, 1959).

SOURCE. Lester G. Crocker, *An Age of Crisis: Man and World in Eighteenth-
Century French Thought* (Baltimore: John Hopkins Press, 1959). Reprinted
by permission of the publisher and the author.

AN AGE OF CRISIS: MAN AND WORLD IN
EIGHTEENTH-CENTURY FRENCH THOUGHT

The eighteenth century was in several ways a turning point in our cultural history. It was an age in which the streams of the past were gradually infiltrated by new facts, new meanings and new attitudes. Turbulence and confusion resulted. The absolute, the essential and the rational swerve toward the relative, the existential and the empirical, in a disordered mixture. A new positivistic outlook denounces hypotheses and mathematical *a prioris;* yet, unable to find explanations and solutions according to its own methodology, this positivism supposes and imagines what it cannot observe, and uses the very rationalistic approach it condemns. The supernatural is submerged by the natural. Science allies the empirical and the rational, seeking, in the historical particular, the essential of law. Anthropology triumphs over metaphysics, psychology over logic. Reason and sentiment are locked in endless debate, the more entangled because a sentimentalist, like Rousseau, believes in the value of human reason, properly used, while a supposed empiricist, like Diderot, is suffused with pre-romantic sentiment.

Whereas the physical sciences had already, in the seventeenth century, broken the shackles of the ancient and medieval world-views, and looked at nature objectively, in ethics the inherited faith in an immutable moral order, supported by the Divinity, continued to struggle vigorously, backed by the fear of many men that mankind was about to become entirely lost in a strange and alien world it had not dared to conceive of before. The physical sciences had expelled from the universe considerations based on value and purpose; a cosmic revolution which inevitably had to penetrate into the world of man. The security that came from the consciousness of being sheltered by an inviolable order, an order designed for man and embodying a meaning that in turn gave meaning to human life and aspirations, was forever shaken. This trend was abetted by a nascent revolution in the biological sciences. Life, it appeared, was only an accident of matter's endless transformations, and its changing convolutions were determined by its own built-in dynamism. Already, in the minds of some, the notion of organic evolution was dawning. This discovery was to complete the rout of faith in man's majesty and security, and in the whole inherited conceptual framework in which he had pictured himself, by ironically changing his origin from God-sprung to a humiliating unfolding of lower forms.

But other men were not afraid. They were determined to face the naked reality of their true place. They were further resolved to apply the empirical method to ethics, and to find a way in which they could live without illusion, and yet live as moral beings, convinced that in the long run a moral order must be of man, and for man. A new courage was now necessary, for whether or not they realized it, mankind was now embarked on a dangerous journey that would take it to the end of the night.

.   .   .

For man to have a moral life, three conditions are prerequisite. First, there must be an accepted distinction between good and evil, and an obligation to do the good. Second, man must be capable of knowing the good. Finally, he must be capable of doing it. Part of the eighteenth century crisis was the re-discovery and triumph of the idea (at least, in many minds) that moral good and evil exist only for man, and in man, and have no other ontological status or support. To these minds it appeared evident that the essential truth which had to be accepted is that "the ethical is not to be discovered in any form of the world-process." This fact, which may be considered as humanity's greatest title to dignity and to glory, was greeted with dismay in many quarters. Christians denied and denounced it. Deists tried desperately to conserve a moral principle in an infinite, undifferentiated Newtonian universe that had no structure in the medieval sense of a rational and hierarchical cosmos. But even they, for the most part, knew that man now had to find his way without God's help. And the debate over evil showed that the march toward divorcing God and the universe from human values could not be halted. The upshot was that no significant purposes for life could be found in the history of the universe, but only within the life of man himself. The depth of the crisis is at once evident. Man found himself utterly without significance, lost in endless space and time, and simultaneously, the center and end-all of his own little universe, ready to annihilate the world, as Schopenhauer says, to maintain his own self a little longer. The very existence of moral good and evil—that is, of good and evil outside of mere individual sentiency—was challenged, and it became necessary to substantiate their objective reality in other ways. This most of the *philosophes* were confident they could do. But if we put together two of the basic postulates of eighteenth century radical thought, that all acts are indifferent in a universe without an objective or absolute order, and that man, as a non-transcendent element of nature, is solely a part of this order, then the foundations of moral nihilism are assured, and the effort of rational solutions becomes very difficult.

. . .

To be sure, man had his apologists; and the upsurge of pre-romantic sentimentality kept alive, in certain sections of society, the belief in his goodness. Many who criticized him, moreover, were convinced of his excellence, in some regards, and of his potentialities. The opinion entertained by some writers, that he is neither good nor bad innately, may even be considered a kind of optimism, since it implies that his natural egotism can be shaped and directed, by outside forces, to the collective and moral good. But nothing could be more erroneous than to speak, as has often been done, of the "simple, naive optimism" of the Age of Enlightenment, and of its belief in "the fundamental goodness and rationality of man"; or of its unawareness that "civilization was a thin and precarious crust," and of its superficial view of human nature that ignored "so many of the deeper and blinder passions both good and bad which inhabit the human heart."

The optimism of the Age of Enlightenment was, for the most part, not about human nature, but about what could be done with human beings, through the progress of science, through education and government, and in general, through the rational reconstruction of society. Its confidence was less in man's reasonableness, than in the power of reason to devise ways of coping with such a creature. This was the hope, but it overlay a substratum of pessimism about man himself. We have seen that many of the writers, on both sides, were aware of man's basic irrationality, and of the reality of radical evil in him (that is, of evil in the core of his personality, his will). We have observed the "will to evil" which forms so strong a current in the novel, and the competitive power drive which underlies Rousseau's philosophy of man in society. Even if men know what is right, the force of their natural instincts is such that they often cannot do the right, or do not want to. The thinkers of the Enlightenment were acutely conscious of the corruption of self-interest in all ideal pretensions of human culture; consequently, their major and continuing effort (except for a few nihilists and anarchists) was to control the workings of that spring of action, by using it to control itself. They did not, as is often claimed, undervalue the power of self-interest; they overestimated the ability of social institutions to effectuate such a control. Perhaps it would be more exact to say that they underestimated the amount of conditioning and coercion that would be required, once a society embarked on such a scheme; and this is what the French Revolution, and later, the Communist revolutions, were to show.

. . .

The makers of the Revolution were representatives of the moderate, deistic current, which had won the allegiance of the vast majority of liberals and thinking men, and not of the bolder, more original extremes of materialism, anarchism, or proto-totalitarianism. But it turned out that the pessimists about human nature had been right, after all; that social life is a struggle for self-interest and power; and that to avoid anarchism, the Revolution was obliged to go to the other extreme, and to forge the first model of totalitarian repression and terror.

. . .

Like Condorcet, Robespierre, when the Revolution broke, represented the average liberal state of mind on religious, political and moral questions. A provincial lawyer and an intellectual, nourished on the writings of the *philosophes,* he became their spokesman, their definer and their preacher. His wide popularity grew partly out of the fact that he eloquently expressed the assumptions and the goals which the *philosophes* had made the common property of the middle class.

Robespierre considered himself a moralist. The science of politics, he declared to the Convention, is only that of "putting into laws and administration the moral truths found in the books of the philosophers. . . . What was this morality? He defined it time and again in his speeches. Men are good or evil according to the direction they give their passions. We must conquer our egoistic passions in order to be good citizens. There are two kinds of self-love: one that is vile, "which seeks an exclusive well-being, purchased by the unhappiness of others; the other, generous, *bienfaisant,* which fuses our happiness with the happiness of all. . . ."

These, and similar theories, we are by now well acquainted with. It was this Robespierre who, in 1791, demanded the abolition of the death penalty, as "essentially unjust" and as completely ineffective, "multiplying crimes rather than preventing them." Here is the heart of his plea: "Listen to the voice of justice and of reason; it cries to us that human judgments are never sure enough so that society can put to death a man condemned by other men who are subject to error." And, even in 1792, he fulminated wrathfully against the "frightful doctrine of denunciation," warning the delegates not to raise a temple to fear.

. . .

[Yet] Robespierre carried to totalitarian limits the process of conditioning that was implicit in some of the *philosophes'* theories, and furnished a model for modern collectivist systems. He caused popular clubs to be founded throughout France, in which, by speeches, songs and discussions, ideas and emotions could be manipulated and men trained to self-sacrifice for the public weal. His government sent "commissioners" throughout the land, to "propagate public spirit, watch over the enemies of the Republic, and establish Jacobin clubs. . . ." He realized fully the power of the press, and insisted on effective propaganda, through that medium, in the theatre, and in the other arts. Following Rousseau again, censorship was established. "All journalists who opposed his ideas were labeled as unpatriotic 'impostors' and hence to be suppressed."

. . .

The effective causes of this change were, of course, political and economic, and all who know the history of that stormy time are familiar with them. However, these causes might not have produced the same effects had Robespierre's ideology been different. The eighteenth century writers had announced themselves as moralists, and so did Robespierre. But, as we shall see (and have already glimpsed), it was a morality whose basis was social utility, and not ethical principle; or, to be exact, it made of utility, social and individual, the chief moral principle. Furthermore, a philosophy of totalitarianism was implicit in a political doctrine whose basic tenet was that the collective will was everything. A later day was to reveal even more fully what Niebuhr has called "the demonic fury of fascist politics in which a collective will expresses boundless ambitions," and which testifies to the result of surrender to the collectivity, as the means of securing individual happiness. As the deputy Courtois wrote in 1795, "they were killing individual happiness to create public happiness."

History shows us that in all such situations, the governing party, or group, and most particularly its leader, assumes that it (or he) is the true expression of the collective will. All opponents are "mistaken," and are "enemies," if they persist. All must be conditioned to recognize the popular will, which is really the will which the leaders assert. They must be "forced to be free." Thus power, starting with a process of rationalization and continuing with one of persuasion, reaches the use of force and finally terminates in terror. Never did Robespierre doubt that he represented the true will of the people. In this way, Rousseau's great "solution" for the social-political problem, submission of the individual will to the general will only (that is, abstractly, to itself), instead of to another individual or to a group, turned out, in practice, to be illusory and self-defeating. At the same time, this course of events also proved again the general truth, that the will-to-power never fails to justify itself in moral terms and to claim the sanctity of pure principles; and the eighteenth century, which understood the egoistic corruption of ideals, might not have been unprepared for this. Twentieth century analogies are obvious. In particular, in our own time we see once more how such epithets as "capitalist conspiracy" or "communist conspiracy" tend to take on ever wider applications until they become identified with all opposition to those who hold power.

. . .

The ethical doctrine which the *philosophes* proposed to substitute for objective imperatives cut away both the metaphysical and the moral supports from under itself. By affirming what they perceived to be man's true place in the universe, they loosed the metaphysical moorings and set him adrift. In a piece in *La philosophie dans le boudoir*, "Frenchmen, one further effort if you wish to be republicans," Sade—who was always, regardless of his own errors, the destroyer of human self-delusion and self-blindness—showed that the republic was founded on the murder of Louis XVI, a king ruling by divine right. It was God who was guillotined on January 21, 1793. For Sade this meant that there was no longer any right to forbid crime and evil instincts, or to prevent his proposed universal society of crime. It was the monarchy that had maintained the idea of God, as the support for laws. Sade goes on to justify calumny, theft and murder, and to demand that they be tolerated.

The *philosophes* had drawn no such conclusion, though a few perceived the danger of it. They believed that ethics can and should be independent of the supernatural. Its necessity and justification, both natural and rational, lay within human life itself. Unfortunately, as we shall later see in more detail, the moral support for ethics was also weakened, as a result of their analysis of human nature and their selected norms of value. They relied on self-interest, on the private and public utility, which they hoped to reconcile in a reconstructed society.

All of their hopes were to fail. The perfect social order could never be created, precisely because of the self-interest and the drive for power which they had understood so well. We have seen where the methods of conditioning and repression were to lead. And rationality, which they themselves so often doubted, was not to govern men's actions. The history of the Western world since the French Revolution bears ample witness to the truth of this analysis. The evidence is written in the minds of the men who came after the eighteenth century, in their continuing doubts, in the increasing confusion and pessimism that envelops them, as well as in the crimes and follies of history. It would be absurd, as I have said, to cast any responsibility on the *philosophes* for the complex circumstances which determined later happenings. They cleaned out the débris of the past and unblocked the roads to the future. They did not succeed in showing men the path to a new way of life, as they had hoped, nor in solving the problem which they helped to bring to a new crisis: the moral and political problem of the relations between individuals in a community, and between the individual and the community. But they took a fateful step forward, one which mankind, in the process of its growth, had to take. In so doing, they left a heritage for the future, both precious and dangerous. The old structure was forever broken. Mankind had to create a new one. The one they dreamed of, to put in its place, was built on faith in human potentialities, and on love for their fellow men. We know now what has happened to this glorious hope, which even then covered a basic pessimism about men themselves. When it crashed and burst, and the smoke of illusion was dissipated, all that remained was the pes-

simism, exacerbated by the Freudian psychology, intensified by
an increased awareness of the metaphysical emptiness which the
eighteenth century had indeed experienced, but from which it
hoped to escape through an independent, humanistic affirmation.

2   *Frankel*

*Charles Frankel has been for many years professor of philoso-
phy at Columbia University and active in public affairs, a combination of pursuits altogether appropriate to someone whose
sympathies lie with the Enlightenment.*

In The Case for Modern Man, *Professor Frankel discusses the
role and results of critical intelligence that was preeminent among
the concerns of the Enlightenment and, according to Frankel, the
mark of its modernity. If we have come to grief in the twentieth
century it is not the result of Enlightenment thought, as Crocker
would have it, but of our abandonment of its ideals. In any case,
it is quite unhistorical to treat ideas as if they were without roots
in history, and were by themselves responsible for subsequent
events. Frankel would have us use Enlightenment ideas in the
new situation that is ours today, as guides to action, which is all
the* philosophes *intended them to be.*

THE CASE FOR MODERN MAN

For three hundred years or more the Western world has been
the scene of a revolution which has become a world revolution.
It is the revolution which made the present era aware that it is
modern—impatient of received dispensations, proud of its enlightenment and powers, and convinced that the world is not the

SOURCE. Charles Frankel, *The Case for Modern Man,* abridged from pp.
1–2, 54–57, 69–71, 85–86, 92–93, 101–102, 106–110, 206–209. Copyright © 1955,
1956 by Charles Frankel. Reprinted by permission of Harper & Row,
Publishers, Inc.

scene for the chastisement of man but the raw material for his arts and his intelligence. The prophets who tell us that this revolution of modernity has been a failure are many. They say that the disasters of recent history have demonstrated that the human reason is the prey of darker forces or higher mysteries, that men cannot be trusted to choose their values for themselves, that history follows a pattern which human beings cannot understand or master. When Prometheus gave us a portion of reason, they say, he was not our benefactor but our tempter.

. . .

What is it about the liberal approach to human affairs that has led to this belief—now so widespread—that liberalism cannot give men the strength of conviction they need to live in this world, and that it undermines the very foundations of social authority? A moment's attention to some recent intellectual history will help us to understand.

Since the early part of the nineteenth century, it is unquestionable that most philosophies of a liberal bent have been, to use the current expression, "relativistic" in their approach to all moral codes and social systems. They have denied, that is to say, that there are any eternal moral principles which are unquestionable, or any immutable standards by which all men and all societies can be judged. In any system of values, for a philosophical "relativist," there is an element of simple preference or interest which cannot be eliminated by argument; and so in any moral system there is always something accidental or personal or limited, something wholly a-rational, which is "relative" to a man's tastes or to the special historical circumstances of a specific place or time. So there cannot be any single system of morals or politics which holds good for everyone; and there cannot be any special group of experts who can lay down the infallible last word on questions of value.

The primary social motive behind this liberal relativism is plain—it is a highly useful tool for unseating the fixed absolutes by which defenders of the *status quo* perennially try to discredit proposals for reform. It has been encouraged as well by the peculiar heterogeneity of modern society and by its mobility—by the welter of different classes, creeds, and occupations that now come together in our cities, by the rapidity with which traditions are replaced, manners changed, and styles put on and off, and by the unprecedented degree to which individuals have been able to move around in space and up and down on the social ladder. But behind the rise of this philosophy there have also been a number of impressive and radical intellectual developments. The first of these stems largely from the philosophy of the eighteenth-century Scottish thinker, David Hume. Hume pointed out that moral statements—statements which tell us how men *should* behave—cannot possibly be proved by pure logic or by an appeal to facts alone. It is also necessary to appeal to human emotions, and particularly to the sentiment of fellow-feeling and sympathy. Moral principles, therefore, cannot be "true" in the way that arithmetic can be true or physics can be true.

The relativistic approach to human values thus stimulated was further encouraged by influences emanating from an independent quarter—the development, in the nineteenth century, of the biological sciences, and of an evolutionary and historical approach to human affairs. These influences, culminating in Marx and Freud, led men to stress the role of ideas and moral values as the selective, practical responses of a vital creature to its environment, and as agencies for adapting human life to changing circumstances. While these new doctrines argued a point which is logically quite different from Hume's, they nevertheless served greatly to reinforce the notion of the relativity of moral codes and social systems. Finally, the *coup de grâce* to the belief in absolutes was given by developments in mathematics and logic which showed that even the so-called "self-evident axioms," cherished for centuries as models of the irrefutable, were in fact matters of human choice and, to a certain extent, of human convenience.

The relativistic philosophy which has resulted from these developments, it is unarguable, has dominated liberal intellectual circles for at least a century. Values have not been regarded as eternal verities about which human beings have no choice. They are the expressions of human preferences, and have a psychological and social setting and an historical career. If there are any moral standards, according to this philosophy, it is human beings who make them. If there is any meaning to history, it is human beings who put it there. To the extent that liberalism has been allied with an empirical outlook in philosophy, it has adopted this view; and to the extent that it has attempted to organize modern society on the basis of purely secular considerations, it has put this view increasingly into practice.

Philosophical relativism is thus the product of significant and serious ideas, and in its foundations is something quite different from the popular attitude of indifference to proof and to truth expressed by the phrase, "Everything is a matter of opinion." And yet, in its general shape and temper this philosophical relativism seems so close to the popular relativism around us, to the confusions and doubts about moral standards and to the simple indifference to morality, that it is easy to see why it should be regarded as the systematic expression of moral skepticism or moral apathy. And this impression has been encouraged by a great many persons who, at some remove from the actual arguments on which philosophical relativism is based, have heard the words of this philosophy without understanding its music.[1]

. . .

I think it is plain that if we are plagued by doubts and uncertainties, they are not the logical consequences of liberal philosophy. Our trouble is not the denial of absolutes; our cure is not a return to the eternal verities. A view of human history which makes man the carrier and ultimate standard of whatever values are found in history neither poisons the springs of the moral life nor undermines the foundations of social authority. But we are faced, then, with the question of how the notion has arisen—and why it is so widely believed—that the modern liberal outlook has corrosive effects on our moral and political convictions. The answer to this question suggests the essential issue that is at stake between those who take a point of view toward modern history like Professor Maritain's and those who share the liberal outlook.

There can be no doubt that a philosophy which holds that all human values are fallible will promote inquiry into existing social arrangements in a way in which an absolutistic philosophy will not. And it is obvious as well that when such inquiry takes place, it may yield the conclusion that some of these social arrangements, or even most of them, do not have the value it is

---

[1] Mussolini, or his philosophical ghost writer, used to say, for example, that Fascism was philosophical relativism in action. Many who do not think highly of Mussolini's politics apparently think highly enough of his philosophical talents to take this statement at face value.

alleged they have. So men's belief in the legitimacy of the existing order is undoubtedly weakened. They no longer believe that it has in all respects a rightful or unqualified claim to be obeyed, or, in other words, that it has as much authority as it claims to have. And it is undeniable that a relativistic philosophy encourages this state of affairs. This is the solid element in the idea that a relativistic philosophy weakens social authority. It does; it weakens the hold of institutions which do not serve the ideals of their members.

But, as Damon Runyon might have said, is this bad? What is needed under these conditions is social reform, and not a dirge on the loss of faith. To blame a relativistic philosophy when men stop believing that their social institutions serve legitimate ideals is a most curious procedure, and hides a quite extraordinary value judgment. If it is discovered that a social order causes avoidable suffering or fails to satisfy interests that could be satisfied, this state of affairs is not the result of the inquiry which reveals it. It is the fault of the social order. There is a natural tendency in most of us to be a little angry with the dentist when his probe touches a sensitive spot in a decayed tooth. I am afraid that Professor Maritain's assertion that the denial of absolutes is "the cause" of the decline of authority in the modern world is a case of blaming the dentist.

Liberalism, in a word, did not come into the modern world to undermine the foundations of authority. It came into the modern world to bring a new kind of authority to social institutions— an authority that rests, not on the a priori arguments of a philosophy or on the ex cathedra statements of those who claim a special access to eternal truths, but on the tested capacity of these institutions to serve living human interests. These words now sound banal; but it is such a conception of authority that the appeal to absolutes would replace. And when this conception of authority was introduced it represented a revolutionary venture in social organization, a new notion of how men ought properly to be related to the societies in which they live.

The new conception of social authority which was introduced by modern liberalism was a part of the general attempt of liberalism to take a social ethic whose classic sanctions had been religious and to reformulate it on a secular basis. Such an attempt is a very radical adventure in the organization of society, and is bound to have its difficulties. It entails a conception of authority which puts men's social arrangements under a more constant test, and inevitably implies a greater tension and strain in society. It means that men see the social systems under which they live as human arrangements, as options to which there are alternatives. It puts the rulers of society under constant pressure to meet new demands. It makes it more difficult to maintain fixed social positions or fixed ideas. Finally, it runs against the whole weight of the absolutistic traditions of the West, and of the unconscious habits of thought and sentiment which those traditions have left with us. There can be no doubt that we have not yet entirely accepted it intellectually, and that only relatively slight pressure is needed to make us yearn for older and more orthodox styles of thought.

. . .

An entire generation of thinkers and writers—New Conservatives and New Liberals—has rediscovered the truth in the ancient doctrine of original sin. The adventure of modern liberalism began with the dream of human perfectibility; it has ended, they point out, in a spectacle of human wickedness raised to a new level of sophistication and efficiency. And this awful denouncement has proved that liberalism was wrong about the one thing about which it is supremely important for a social movement to be right—human nature itself. This is the basic and insoluble problem.

When there is evil in the world, we are reminded, it is not just the result of social institutions or human ignorance. It comes from something deeper and more enduring—a perversity in the human soul itself. When the human intellect errs, this is not just the result of human fallibility, but of human egoism and pride; when there is injustice or cruelty in society, this mirrors a maliciousness in the human spirit. Liberalism, with its faith in human intelligence and its zeal for improving social conditions, did not see what the illiberal Dostoevsky, with his more-than-rational wisdom, was able to see—"the underground man" who has come to the surface in the twentieth century. As a result liberals and men of good will have been unable to understand, or to stand up to, the hard realities of life in this century. "Cursed is the man who has faith in man," the maxim of Jeremiah, has emerged as a new touchstone of political realism.

. . .

The liberal belief in the perfectibility of man, says Mr. Niebuhr, is the single article of faith which has most distinguished
modern culture. It is responsible for the follies, self-deceptions,
and arrogant hopes on which the modern era has misspent its
energies. List the characteristic weaknesses of the liberal mind—
its futile pursuit of purity in politics, its conviction that history is
a struggle between the enlightened and the unenlightened, its
faith in objective reason and its conviction that there is such a
thing as disinterested good will—and we see the practical consequences of the liberal approach to history. The belief in the
natural goodness of man explains why modern liberals were so
late in recognizing the true nature of Fascism. The belief that evil
is social in its origins and can be eliminated by changing society
explains why so many have been seduced by Communism. The
belief that when man progresses in knowledge he also progresses
in virtue explains why science has been erected into a false Mes-
siah. The liberal faith that everything will be washed clean by
the waters of time explains why modern liberalism has had a
manic-depressive character, moving from bouts of utopian enthusiasm at one extreme to bouts of startled disillusion and
despair at the other. Never has a social movement allowed itself
such exorbitant hopes, or placed such faith in human nature and
human reason; and never, as a result, have the hopes of any social
movement been so completely and terrifyingly refuted by events.
"In one century," Mr. Niebuhr observes, "modern man had
claimed to have achieved the dizzy heights of the mastery both
of natural processes and historical destiny. In the following century he is hopelessly enmeshed in an historical fate, threatening
mutual destruction, from which he seems incapable of extricating
himself. A word of Scripture fits the situation perfectly: 'He that
sitteth in the heavens shall laugh: the Lord shall have them in
derision.' "

.   .   .

But exactly what have our illusions been?
Liberalism, it is said on all sides, has forgotten to take human
egoism into account, and has been utopian in its conception of
what can be made of man. This picture of liberalism has become
one of the standing commonplaces of current discussion, and is
shared by the New Liberal and the New Conservative alike.
"Practically all schools of modern culture," says Mr. Niebuhr,

". . . are united in denying the obvious fact that all men are persistently inclined to regard themselves more highly and are more assiduously concerned with their own interests than any 'objective' view of their importance would warrant." But the belief in the undying egoism of human beings, and the persistence in any society of the struggle for power, has in fact been the distinguishing feature of the liberal approach to politics. "The principle of human nature, upon which the necessity of government is founded, the propensity of one man to possess himself of the objects of desire at the cost of another, leads on, by infallible sequence, not only to that degree of plunder which leaves the members (except the instruments and recipients) the bare means of subsistence, but to that degree of cruelty which is necessary to keep in existence the most intense terrors." These are not Mr. Niebuhr's words. They are the words of James Mill, the liberal and utilitarian, writing on the foundations of government. The idea that philosophical liberalism has been committed to a perfectionist theory of human nature is in fact a parody of liberal thought.

In general, the British liberal tradition has taken most of its ideas on the behavior of political man from Thomas Hobbes, who described man as *homo lupus*—a predatory animal. Even those figures who, like John Locke, have taken a more genial view of human nature, have nevertheless regarded the irrepressible tendency of each man to favor his own cause as a major reason for substituting a politically organized society for "the state of nature." And in the twentieth century, that arch exemplar of liberalism is thought and action, Bertrand Russell, has tried to base an entire political theory on the strength, uneliminability, and remarkable variety of men's demands for power. Nor is it only British liberalism that does not fit the portrait that is now drawn of classic liberalism. The philosophers of the French Enlightenment are repeatedly described as boundless optimists and visionaries. But is it really possible to say of Rousseau who wrote the *Confessions,* or Diderot who wrote *Rameau's Nephew,* or Voltaire who wrote *Candide,* that they entertained great illusions either about their own goodness or the goodness of other men? Even the philosopher Helvetius, who was most extreme in his hopes about what could be done with human nature, and who was looked upon as a little strange by most of his liberal contemporaries, wrote: "In order to love mankind, we must expect little from them."

.   .   .

If we judge the liberal philosophy of history by its most representative spokesman, the belief in the progress of man was not made up out of whole cloth, and the men who held it were not suffering from an *idée fixe* about human goodness which prevented them from recognizing plain facts. In Condorcet's hands, the belief in the perfectibility of man was really a belief better translated into English as a belief in the *improvability* of man. And the ideals it projected point the way to our crucial problems, and give us a framework that is still valid for our social thinking.

That Condorcet's enthusiasm was aroused by this vision, and that many liberal writers in the eighteenth and nineteenth centuries (and an even greater number of illiberal ones) were stimulated by it into utopian or quasi-utopian dreams is undeniable. They lived in the fine glow of a major revolution in human affairs, and they recognized this revolution for what it was. If they were overly optimistic, it was a matter of mood and temper and circumstance. It was not a matter of fundamental philosophic principle. To take a patronizing attitude toward the men who held these dreams is to reveal a failure of historical imagination. For these men were living through a scientific and technological revolution which gave promise that for the first time in human history men would be able to get off their backs in the struggle with nature—that men could finally, to put it in unadorned terms, eat adequately and live in reasonable comfort and health. To have been dazzled by the prospects which this revolution held forth is not only understandable; more, the men who were dazzled, and who wrote the passages at which the New Pessimists now scoff, were performing the important function of announcing the new possibilities for the moral and intellectual improvement of mankind which this very real material revolution had set loose. In the light of what was contained in human experience up to that time, to do this took courage and imagination; and not to have done it would have been a greater error, a more sizable failure to provide directing ideas to modern culture, than to have played the old tune of original sin.

There is, in fact, a quite fundamental confusion in the idea that the liberal doctrine of "the goodness of man" reveals an impossibly naïve theory of human nature. It is a confusion between a scheme of moral values and a psychological theory. The slogan, "the goodness of man," is indeed an alternative to the doctrine of original sin. But it is not primarily an alternative description of human behavior; it is an alternative frame of moral reference— a dramatic device for freeing practical questions of politics or historical explanation from control by the ideal of salvation and the value judgments that follow from it.

For the doctrine of original sin defines "good" and "evil" with respect to the final goal of personal salvation. By calling man "evil" or "sinful," it means to say that man, through his own efforts alone, cannot be immortal, or free his mind or soul from dependence on a corrupt body, or be infallible in his intellectual judgments, or perfectly saintly in his behavior. And liberal philosophers would have agreed with all of these statements of fact. What they were doing in speaking about "the goodness of man" was simply to assert the legitimacy of talking about human traits in some other context than this context of sin and redemption. From the point of view of being saved from sin, for example, egoism might be evil; but from an economic point of view it might be good as a pivot for ambition; or from a political point of view it might be good as a defense against despotism; or, indeed, it might be neither good nor bad, but simply what has to be taken into account in governing human affairs. "Moralists declaim continually against the badness of men," wrote Helvetius, "but this shows how little they understand of this matter. Men are not bad; they are merely subject to their own interests." It is this "transvaluation of values," this introduction of a new context for the assessment of human traits, which is involved in statements about "the goodness of man."

It is Mr. Niebuhr's failure to see this point which explains his caricature of liberal views of human nature. On Mr. Niebuhr's accounting, Hobbes and Locke, Hume and Rousseau, rationalists and romantics, all turn out to have entertained essentially the same overestimate of the "goodness" of man. But it is plain that if there is anything that unites these men, it is not a psychological theory, nor even a common set of value judgments; it is only a common disposition to place whatever value judgments they make in a humanistic setting, to refuse to impose standards on man which are irrelevant to what he wants and what he can do. The

liberal attack on the doctrine of original sin was a phase in the
transition of social thinking from preoccupation with the classic
problem of "theodicy"—the justification of God's ways to man—
to a preoccupation with concrete, individual problems in morals
and society. It set the problem of man's transcendent perversity
aside; it set the problem of man's other-worldly destiny aside; it
dropped the question of salvation out of the group of questions
which must be examined before a social program can be developed. In arguing for the possibility of greater happiness in
human affairs, philosophical liberals were not talking about redemption through history. They were not talking about redemption at all. For "happiness" is not a synonym for "salvation," and
"progress" is not a synonym for the journey of the soul to God.

But if the difference between a belief in the goodness of man
and a belief in original sin is mainly a difference in the mood
with which we approach human affairs and the language we employ to discuss them, it is a difference which has tremendous practical consequences for political strategy and for the quality of a
culture.

. . .

It is a difference that is important. For there were, and are,
other motives as well behind talking about "the goodness of man"
instead of "the sinfulness of man." The dictum that "man is good"
changed the initial questions with which social thinkers began
their work. It gave the first move to the reformer, and shifted the
burden of proof to those who wished to say that human pain
was necessary or desirable. For human intelligence and energy
have been consistently diverted from dealing with specific evils
and specific pains by generalizations to the effect that Evil is inherent in human nature and Pain is its merited punishment. The
philosophes of the eighteenth century and the Philosophic Radicals of the nineteenth century came into a world entangled in a
mass of verbal rituals, authorities descended from the past, high-
sounding abstractions, and immeasurable human wretchedness.
In talking about "the goodness of man" they were demanding
that man's living interests be taken seriously, and that human
pain be regarded as a problem initially inviting compassion and
practical effort, and not higher dialectics about its necessity. This
notion that existing human preferences should be consulted in
determining social arrangements may now seem a trivial plati-

tude. But as a concrete proposal for reassessing existing social arrangements, it has usually been greeted with massive indifference, and not infrequently with active hostility. If it is now a platitude, we have the idea of the goodness of man to thank for it. It was an essential instrument in the domesticating of reform in Western society.

.   .   .

It would be absurd to deny (though it is done every day in four-color advertisements) that the hopes which the liberal outlook on history expressed have not been disappointed. But before we decide that it was these hopes that misled us, it would be well to look at the nature and quality of the disappointments we have suffered. For there is something quite distinctive about them. It suggests how very new and special these disappointments are, and what the context is in which they have arisen. And it suggests, too, that our disappointments, while real, need not be final.

There is an obvious fact about recent history which it is easy to forget. We have had wars which have involved whole populations as have no wars in the past, depressions which have left a third of the working population unemployed, and political tyrannies whose power to penetrate into the daily lives of individuals puts all past tyrannies in the shade; we live now with weapons that threaten the sheer physical survival of the race, weapons we have invented but are not quite sure we know how not to use. And yet on certain simple standards of progress, progress in the last hundred and fifty years has been unprecedented. Basic conditions of human life have changed for the better, and almost beyond recognition. The average length of life has been steadily extended; illiteracy has been progressively eliminated; leisure time has grown; work, while much of it is routine, mechanical, and dispiriting, is at least less back-breaking; a certain degree of uniformity and equity has been introduced into our legal systems; special privilege, while great, is now recognized as special privilege. These may be limited indices of human progress, but only the most improbable callousness could altogether neglect them. In these respects, men's lives have changed more radically in the last hundred and fifty years than in all history before that time.

This progress throws our present disappointments into perspective. For the simple fact is that men's happiness depends upon their expectations—and the expectations of modern men have grown tremendously. This is the setting in which our present sense that we are going to the dogs must be understood. If there is now a widespread sense of guilt and failure, it is in part because humanitarian feelings have increased, and because the moral sympathies of many ordinary men and women now have an immeasurably greater scope than the sympathies of any but the most exceptional leaders of mankind in the past. If there is a sense that we in this century have a peculiar talent for sin, it is because the collective disasters we have suffered are almost all of them clearly man-made—a token of human power which represents a quite new state of affairs in human experience. If the existence of poverty oppresses us, it is because we do not think it is inevitable. If intellectual inquisitions shock our sensibilities, and seem like inexplicable eruptions of irrationality, it is because our moral expectations have been profoundly altered by the prestige which institutions of free inquiry now enjoy. And if we are worried about the chances of the human race for survival, this is painful, but it is a little like the gout. Most men in the past, most men in Asia and Africa today, have had to worry about their own short-run personal survival.

Indeed, the very bitterness with which we contemplate the difference between our expectations and our actual performance has arisen within this context. There is bound to be some difference between the professions and the actual practice of any society; in most societies this difference has been very large. But this gap between theory and practice has been what most men in the past have expected. It is precisely what their absolutistic moral codes explained and justified. The steady development of an experimental attitude toward morals and society in the modern era has meant, in contrast, that men expect human ideals and human practices to be closer together. It means that they demand that myths and symbols stand for some reality. And it has subjected both our ideals and our institutions to a more constant test, and has made it harder to maintain a gap between theory and practice without insupportable tensions.

In short, there is a sense in which the philosophies of history we have studied are right. Our present complaints have arisen within the context of a secular society, a pervasive science and technology, and a liberal outlook on human history. But those who blame this outlook for our problems are taking the very context in which we define these problems and converting it into their cause. It is like saying that the invention of arithmetic is the cause of Junior's troubles at school.

For the revolution of modernity has not been only a material revolution or an intellectual revolution. It has been a moral revolution of extraordinary scope, a radical alteration in what the human imagination is prepared to envisage and demand. And it has changed the basic dimensions in which we measure happiness and unhappiness, success and failure. It has given us the sense that we make our own history; it has led us to impose new and more exacting demands on ourselves and our leaders; it has set loose the restless vision of a world in which men might be liberated from age-old burdens, and come to set their own standards and govern their own lives.

To be "modern" is not a monopoly of modern man. There have been modern men in most eras, and there have been other modern eras. At least once before, during the Greek Enlightenment, the Western mind envisaged a world in which the critical spirit would be preferred over the pious spirit, and in which doubt, not dogma, would be regarded as the leaven of a high civilization. Such modernity has been only one strain in the present era, and not always a dominant one. But it has lasted longer, gone deeper, and spread farther than has the modern spirit in any other time. No other age has gone so far in the belief that the spirit of modernity might be widely shared, and that all men might participate in the goods and responsibilities of a modern civilization. The modern spirit in Athens was a brief and glimmering thing, arising in a society based on slavery. The modern spirit in fifteenth-century Italy was an aristocratic phenomenon, limited to an elite. But our own revolution of modernity has led to the unprecedented vision of a society in which the opportunity for personal achievement and social power would be generally diffused among men, and not limited to a selected group.

And as its crowning symbol, it developed a radically new outlook on human destiny, which saw the meaning of history in terms of the progress of the human mind, and held that human history could be made to follow the direction that men chose to give it. Prometheus was the first modern. The revolution of modernity proposed to put men squarely on Prometheus' side. It is a unique venture in human affairs, and we can only relieve the strains and tensions it has created by taking it seriously. Our disappointments are real. But they are real because our powers are great and our expectations legitimately high.

C. CONCLUSION

The Enlightenment—Relevant or Irrelevant

How relevant to us is the Enlightenment? We have moved into a new period of history, which for want of a better word we may call post-modern, and which is altogether different from the Age of Reason. The Enlightenment's social setting is no longer ours. Its values are not our own. What period does it belong to? Some would see it as the end of the Renaissance, or as Becker does, the end of the Middle Ages. Others would see it as the beginning of modern times. It seems reasonable, however, to view it as defining the modern period in history, which had its roots in the seventeenth century (or even earlier) its fruition in the eighteenth, and its fulfillment in the nineteenth century.

The Enlightenment reflected the state of politics and society in the modern period. It consisted essentially of an effort to forge an ethical system related to but not substantially the same as the new scientific experience. It was the creation of the Atlantic Community, largely England and France, and to a lesser degree, Germany. The English gentleman of the eighteenth century was a practical man interested in politics, commerce, and agriculture. With his revolution behind him he had a clear field for action in all three, and ordinarily, when he read philosophy he did so to help him decide issues of immediate importance. He looked to Locke for a rule of political equity, to Hume for a practical theology, and to Adam Smith for the principles of political economy. His scientific empiricism usually led him to emphasize the particular in ethical thought.

Perhaps for want of a nation-state, little interested the German burgher outside his mundane concerns, unless it was religion. The German philosopher therefore tended toward abstract thought, and was inclined as a consequence to favor the universal in ethics. The French on the other hand were faced with practical problems that the realities of politics forced them to objectify. With social discontent rising, the *philosophes* were engaged in matters of vital importance when they challenged privilege, denounced intolerance, and promoted social progress. Men of letters who were denied political experience, they founded their programs on abstract principles. Thus the French stood midway between the English and the Germans in matters of philosophical interest, and tried to have the best of both perspectives—to provide the answer to practical problems through an appeal to universals. It was characteristic of them that they directed their attention in politics toward linking the one and the many, man and society. The typical note in French social thought was sounded by Rousseau who was concerned with each man's freedom, the general will being the standard of individual perfection. Thus individual freedom and social responsibility were linked in an effort to harmonize the citizen and the state and to introduce moral purpose into society.

How are we to assess the Enlightenment? Where the Enlightenment stood for reason, moral freedom, and cosmopolitanism, we are largely irrationalist, behaviorist, and provincial in outlook. The *philosophes* were not detached thinkers, nor were they complacent. They really meant it when they said they were opposed to prejudice, dogmatism, and intolerance. They were deeply concerned to find in man what there was worth supporting, and they acted on their new found belief that men would be better for being free from fear and ignorance when they fought for justice and toleration against thoughtless barbarism and mindless parochialism. Theirs was an age of science. Ours is an age of technocracy that no longer values science. The disinterestedness of science has been confused in our own day with detachment, and its values of rationality and altruism are being sacrificed to a vision of spiritual self-fulfillment. Reason has been identified with industrial efficiency, and we are abandoning both in return for a religion of personal salvation that is meant somehow to bring us together in a universal brotherhood of tender feeling. Some among us would conclude that our irrationalist activism is not going to produce any change worth having, that our behaviorism is an escape from freedom, and that our spiritual innocence is the epitome of quite unromantic hedonism. On the other hand, many would argue that the Enlightenment shallowly emphasized reason to the neglect of unreason, that its vaunted quest for freedom sprang from, and was directed at the Bourgeois few, that its optimistic faith in science was a materialistic one, and its belief in history and humanity an illusion.

The Enlightenment view of freedom did in fact arise with the bourgeoisie—people who lived in cities, as free citizens, and who were not necessarily middle class citizens,—and may be a true view for all that. To declare otherwise is to attach ourselves to ideology when it is knowledge that we seek, which may be no more than arguing in a circle for one of the secular ideals of the Enlightenment. Those secular ideals—tolerance, free thought, rational consent—were spiritual enough, however, to evoke a genuine idealism among men, though we may view them as mere illusion. Doubtless every age has its illusions, perhaps intrinsic to its existence. Ours are just the kind that the Enlightenment sought to ban as being at best millenial, at worst, self-serving. Finally, the Enlightenment praise of reason was a way of thinking, one which has consistently provided new knowledge, even of the irrational, and which at its core is self-critical. Reason if fallible is corrigible; and science is the one orthodoxy that thrives on correction in an on-going process that can look back as well as forward. The *philosophes* understood the connection in history between past and future as giving meaning to their search for scientific and social truth. It has always been a mark of civilized men that they be willing to trust themselves to a continuing enterprise whose outcome is in doubt, but whose value, they believe, lies as much in the search itself as in the result they seek.

BIBLIOGRAPHICAL NOTE

The number of works about the Enlightenment in all its attitudes is enormous. Far fewer are the general works that discuss the Enlightenment as a whole. I have selected some in English that would be useful to the student for inclusion below, together with a few volumes on specific aspects and individuals of the period. For a detailed listing of works see the splendid bibliographies attached to Peter Gay's two recent and readable volumes, *The Enlightenment: An Interpretation*, (New York, 1966–1969).

In addition to those two volumes and others cited elsewhere in this book, there are the following that consider the Enlightenment synoptically.

W. H. Barber, ed., *The Age of Enlightenment* (Edinburgh, 1967).

Alfred Cobban, *In Search of Humanity* (New York, 1960).

Charles Frankel, *The Faith of Reason* (New York, 1969).

Peter Gay, *The Party of Humanity* (New York, 1954).

Norman Hampson, *The Enlightenment* (Baltimore, 1968).

Paul Hazard, *The European Mind* (New York, 1963).

———, *European Thought in the Eighteenth Century* (New York, 1963).

Kingsley Martin, *French Liberal Thought in the Eighteenth Century* (New York, 1963).

Preserved Smith, *The Enlightenment: 1687–1776* (New York, 1962).

E. R. Wasserman, ed., *Aspects of the Eighteenth Century* (Baltimore, 1965).

On particular aspects and individuals of the Enlightenment see the following.

Henry S. Allison, *Lessing and the Enlightenment* (Ann Arbor, 1966).

F. M. Barnard, *Herder's Social and National Thought* (New York, 1965).

J. B. Black, *The Art of History* (New York, 1926).

Louis I. Bredvold, *The Brave New World of the Enlightenment* (Ann Arbor, 1961).

J. B. Bury, *The Idea of Progress* (New York, 1938).

Herbert Butterfield, *The Origins of Modern Science, 1300–1800* (New York, 1951).

Ernest Cassirer, *The Question of Jean-Jacques Rousseau* (Bloomington, 1963).

———, *Rousseau, Kant, and Goethe* (New York, 1945).

Peter Gay, *Voltaire's Politics* (New York, 1965).

Ronald Grimsley, *Jean D'Alembert, 1717–1783* (New York, 1963).

Elie Halévy, *The Growth of Philosophic Radicalism* (Boston, 1955).

A. Rupert Hall, *The Scientific Revolution, 1500–1800: The Formation of the Modern Scientific Attitude* (Boston, 1966).

Thomas L. Hankins, *Jean D'Alembert: Science and the Enlightenment* (London, 1970).

Ronald W. Harris, *Reason and Nature in the Eighteenth Century, 1714–1780* (London, 1968).

Charles W. Hendel, *Jean-Jacques Rousseau, Moralist* (London, 1934).

Robert H. Hurlbutt, *Hume, Newton, and the Design Argument* (Lincoln, 1965).

Isabel Knight, *The Geometric Spirit: The Abbé de Condillac and the French Enlightenment* (New Haven, 1968).

Alexander Koyré, *From the Closed World to the Infinite Universe* (Baltimore, 1968).

Harold J. Laski, *Political Thought in England: Locke to Bentham* (London, 1919).

Frank Manuel, *The Eighteenth Century Confronts the Gods* (New York, 1967).

———, *The Prophets of Paris* (New York, 1962).

Leonard M. Marsak, "Bernard de Fontenelle: The Idea of Science in the French Enlightenment," *Transactions of the American Philosophical Society,* 49 (1959), part 7.

R. R. Palmer, *Catholics and Unbelievers in Eighteenth Century France* (Princeton, 1939).

Philip C. Ritterbush, *Overtures to Biology* (New Haven, 1964).

R. V. Sampson, *Progress in the Age of Reason* (London, 1956).

Robert Shackleton, *Montesquieu* (New York, 1961).

Judith Shklar, *Men and Citizens: A Study of Rousseau's Social Theory* (New York, 1969).

David W. Smith, *Helvétius* (New York, 1965).

Norman Kemp Smith, *The Philosophy of David Hume* (New York, 1941).

Leslie Stephen, *History of English Thought in the Eighteenth Century,* 2 vols. (New York, 1962).

John B. Stewart, *The Moral and Political Philosophy of David Hume* (New York, 1963).

J. L. Talmon, *The Origins of Totalitarian Democracy* (New York, 1960).

Aram Vartanian, *Diderot and Descartes* (Princeton, 1953).

Henry Vyverberg, *Historical Pessimism in the French Enlightenment* (Cambridge, Mass., 1958).

Arthur Wilson, *Diderot: The Testing Years, 1713–1759* (New York, 1957).